# BASIC INFLUENCING SKILLS

## (THIRD EDITION)

**Allen E. Ivey, Norma Gluckstern Packard,
and Mary Bradford Ivey**

Dedication

*To our basic influencers with love and admiration:*

*Miriam and Lloyd Ivey*
*Isabelle and Joseph Kaplan*
*Florence and Rupert Bradford*

Certain parts of this book are taken from the 1994 book *Intentional Interviewing and Counseling* and the 1971 book *Microcounseling: Innovations in Interviewing Training* by Allen E. Ivey. Permission to quote and paraphrase certain portions of the books was granted by the publishers, Brooks/Cole and Charles C. Thomas. Videotapes to accompany this book are available from Microtraining Associates, Inc.

Copyright © 1976, 1984, 1997
Microtraining Associates
An Imprint of Alexander Street Press
3212 Duke Street
Alexandria, VA 22314
phone: 800-889-5937 or 703-212-8520
website: http://www.emicrotraining.com
email: info@emicrotraining.com
ISBN-13: 978-0-917276-04-0
ISBN-10: 0-917276-04-3

# CONTENTS

# CONTENTS

# CHAPTER 1

## INTRODUCTION AND OVERVIEW

Imagine that someone has come to you for help.

> Client:  My parents are really difficult. It looks like they are headed for divorce. Dad just moved out and Mom's a disaster. I think he's got a friend. Mom just sits and cries and seems to want me to take over. And here I am in my first year of college. I wish I didn't live at home, but this is the only way I can make it. I work fifteen hours a week and am just barely making grades. But, now I find myself so upset, I can't study. And, then there is my sister . . . (the story continues).

Most likely you know someone who has experienced all of the above and parts of the story may be personally familiar. What are you going to do to help this student make sense of and deal with these issues? Take a moment below and write how you would respond to this client.

_____

_____

_____

_____

If possible, compare your ideas of helping responses with those of others. You will likely find that people think about and respond to the same story quite differently. And, you may also note that more than one response may be helpful.

## WHAT THIS BOOK OFFERS YOU

One of the major objectives of this book is to help you increase the number of possible responses you can offer clients or helpees. Your own first ideas for what to say are important, but if your original helping comments don't work, it is important to have many other possibilities to reach those whom you would help.

If you actively engage in the reading, observation, and practice exercises of this book, you will have the following abilities:

1. *Ability to enable clients or helpees tell their stories in their own language and fashion.* You will be able to draw out the facts, feelings, and organization of your helpees' stories.

2. *Ability to generate an infinite number of helping responses.* Rather than seeking one "correct" or "best" way to respond, anticipate increased flexibility.

3. *Ability to demonstrate influencing skills in the interview.* Each skill will be presented with ample opportunity for mastery.

4. *Ability to conduct a well-formed five-stage interview.* A basic structure for interviewing is presented that is useful for many different types of helping sessions.

5. *Ability to engage in assertiveness training.* One important strategy of the counseling profession is enabling clients to speak up for themselves in an appropriate manner that is neither too soft nor too aggressive.

There are nine specific skills and strategies in this book listed below. Within each skill area are multiple possibilities to enable you to expand your response capability.

The nine segments of *Basic Influencing Skills* and Strategies include the following:

| Skill Area | Definition | Function in the Interview |
|---|---|---|
| Basic Listening Sequence and Positive Asset Search | An integrated review of basic attending skills | Demonstrates to the helpee that you are listening. Helps organize the facts and feelings of the client's narrative story. The positive asset search is critical for solution of concerns and problems. |
| Focusing | Selectively attending to the full complexity of a helpee's concern | Enables you and the helpee to view the issue from a variety of perspectives. Particularly important in discovering how family and cultural issues may relate to the story and its possible resolution. |
| Confrontation | Noting incongruity in helpee issues and presentation | Facilitates client self-exploration and problem solving. When confronted effectively, many helpees resolve their own concerns. |
| Directives | Providing the client with a concrete action | Enables the client to think in new ways about the situation and, often, to generate new ways of acting. |
| Self-Disclosure and Feedback | Sharing your experiences and letting the client know how others are seeing her or him | These two skills provide the helpee with an opportunity to see how stories and issues are viewed by others. These skills are often helpful in client self-examination and evaluation. |
| Reframing/ Interpretation | Provides an alternative frame of reference to view an issue or situation | Stimulates creative problem-solving on the part of the client. A new way of viewing the situation may change thinking, feeling, and behavior. The narrative takes on a new meaning. |
| Skill Integration I Five-Stage Interview Structure | Provides specifics for integrating skills in a well-formed interview | The five stages of the interview: 1. rapport/structuring; 2. gathering information and accessing positive assets; 3. goal setting; 4. exploring alternatives; and 5. generalization of the interview to daily life. |
| Skill Integration II Assertiveness Training | Microskills Five-stage interview model adapted for assertiveness training | Provides the helpee with a concrete way to examine and change behavior. |
| Teaching Skills | Using the strategies of this book as a teaching method | Many clients will benefit from direct instruction in communication skills. In addition, a major role of the helper is conducting workshops in helping skills. Chapter 9 shows how to teach microskills. |

## NARRATIVE AND SKILLS: REWRITING CLIENT STORIES

The student's story at the beginning of this chapter was full of issues and concerns. The narrative approach to interviewing and counseling seeks to help people tell their stories. Just having our life stories heard by another person is a powerful and empowering experience. With some clients, just listening to the story line empathically and warmly is enough.

Others, however, need new stories, fresh ways to think about themselves, and more effective methods to act to change their lives. For example, the overwhelmed student may be telling us a story of lack of control. We can help that student rewrite that story by prioritizing issues, making decisions about what can and cannot be done, and providing new ways for the student to think about self and others. The new underlying story line may become, "I am indeed stressed, but I need to take care of myself if I am to help my family. I can't change everything, but I can do some things to make it better."

Through the effective use of listening and influencing skills, we can help clients make sense of their lives and stories—and then to act to change things. The influencing skills described in this book all focus on ways which can enable helpees to think and act differently.

The client on page one expressed many problems in the story. What are some positive ways you can imagine her rewriting her story and issues?

_____

_____

_____

_____

## MICROTRAINING AS A WAY TO TEACH SKILLS AND STRATEGIES

*Basic Influencing Skills* seeks to increase your helping alternatives via a method termed "microtraining." Here you will find the interview broken down into component parts which can be studied and mastered one at a time. Microtraining uses a straightforward, concrete system and presents specific skills of interviewing via the following format:

> 1. *Brief warm-up or introduction to the skill or strategy.* For example, the story at the beginning of this chapter is designed to help us all think about multiple ways of responding to client stories.

> 2. *Reading about the skill or strategy.* In this book, you will find brief and highly specific ideas which are designed to clarify the helping process.

> 3. *Viewing the skill or strategy.* A series of videotapes accompany this book, but they are not essential. What is important in learning the skills of interviewing is seeing someone engage in actual practice. Thus, you may see one of Microtraining's videos, one made by your instructor or workshop leader, or perhaps even a live demonstration by your leader or co-participants in your class or workshop. Seeing the skill in action is important.

> 4. *Practice.* You will be asked to practice the skill or strategy. Reading about or seeing a skill is only a beginning. You will be asked to practice the single strategy in small groups so that you can demonstrate that you can use the strategy in the interview successfully.

> 5. *Generalization.* Finally, microtraining asks you to take the skill or strategy out to the "real world" and incorporate it into interviewing practice. Learning in the classroom is not enough.

Microtraining organizes helping skills in a pyramid or hierarchy (see Figure 1). Basic to the microskills hierarchy is the idea that one builds on a foundation of solid learning and expertise and gradually moves towards full competence in interviewing, helping, or counseling. Think about yourself as a possible teacher of skills.

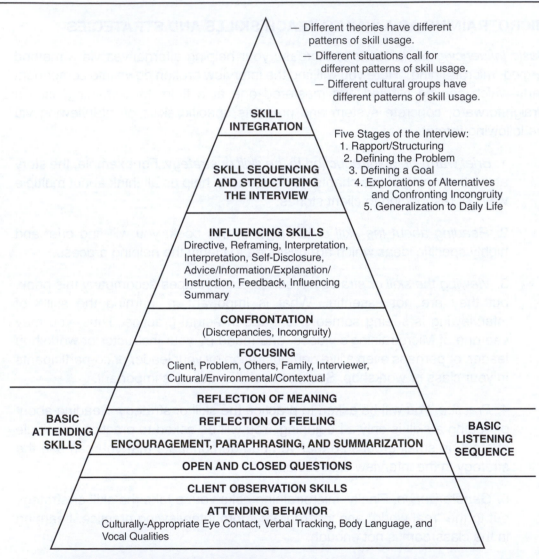

— Different theories have different patterns of skill usage.

— Different situations call for different patterns of skill usage.

— Different cultural groups have different patterns of skill usage.

**SKILL INTEGRATION**

Five Stages of the Interview:
1. Rapport/Structuring
2. Defining the Problem
3. Defining a Goal
4. Explorations of Alternatives and Confronting Incongruity
5. Generalization to Daily Life

**SKILL SEQUENCING AND STRUCTURING THE INTERVIEW**

**INFLUENCING SKILLS**
Directive, Reframing, Interpretation, Interpretation, Self-Disclosure, Advice/Information/Explanation/ Instruction, Feedback, Influencing Summary

**CONFRONTATION**
(Discrepancies, Incongruity)

**FOCUSING**
Client, Problem, Others, Family, Interviewer, Cultural/Environmental/Contextual

**REFLECTION OF MEANING**

**REFLECTION OF FEELING**

**ENCOURAGEMENT, PARAPHRASING, AND SUMMARIZATION**

**OPEN AND CLOSED QUESTIONS**

**CLIENT OBSERVATION SKILLS**

**ATTENDING BEHAVIOR**
Culturally-Appropriate Eye Contact, Verbal Tracking, Body Language, and Vocal Qualities

**BASIC ATTENDING SKILLS**

**BASIC LISTENING SEQUENCE**

1. Attending behavior and client observation skills form the foundation of effective communication, but are not always the appropriate place to begin training.
2. The basic listening sequence of attending skills (open and closed questions, encouraging, paraphrasing, reflection of feeling, and summarization) is often found in effective interviewing, management, social work, physician diagnostic sessions, and many other settings.

**FIGURE 1.** The Microskills Hierarchy. Copyright 1982, 1995 Allen E. Ivey. Box 641. N. Amherst, Mass. 01059.

## DETERMINING YOUR OWN PERSONAL STYLE

Microtraining emphasizes competencies, skills, and the ability to influence the world. Yet, the most important thing that comes out of successful training in microcounseling is a helper who is both competent and clear about his or her actions in the helping session, is directly concerned with value issues, and is able to decide which skills are appropriate within an individual theoretical framework.

Your task in this book is to experiment with the several skills and to determine those which "fit" you most comfortably. Some are natural to you already; others will come to you with more difficulty. Throughout this training, you must evaluate each skill area and decide whether this skill is compatible with you and your world view.

Our firm belief is that the individual helper must decide on the helping style in which maximum comfort and effectiveness are achieved. So, although you are bombarded in helping training programs with theories, ideas, and skills, it is you who must decide what type of helper to be. From beginning to end, examine yourself and the materials and make your own decision as to what you want to be.

While it is vital that you find your own space as a volunteer or professional helper, comfort and selecting one's own style may not be sufficient. Just because you favor a certain skill, strategy, or theory does not mean that the client does as well. Thus, it becomes necessary that you "push the envelope" and learn new ways of relating to clients even though they may not be fully comfortable to you at the beginning.

## MASTERY GOALS

The skills in this book may be learned to differing levels of competence. The first level of learning is demonstrated when you are able to classify and *identify* the several helping leads of microcounseling. The second level occurs when you are able to use specific skills in the practice interview. These first two levels are called *identification mastery* and *basic mastery*.

*Active mastery* is a third level of particular importance. We have found that many people can learn to identify skills and demonstrate them in a role-played interview. These identification and basic levels are vital. However, what really makes a difference is your ability to take these skills and strategies into real interviews and use them with positive client effect.

When seeking active mastery, ask yourself two questions:

Am I actually using the skill or strategy in the interview?

Are my clients changing their thoughts, emotions, or actions as a result of what we are doing together?

Active mastery asks you to look carefully at your impact in the interview. Are you making a difference?

However, active mastery does not imply helper control or direction of client thoughts, feelings, or actions. The goal of active mastery is to help clients sort out their own wishes and desires. Counselor active mastery is to be used as a tool to facilitate client-directed action. If a client does not respond to an interviewer lead or statement (or act on a decision beyond the interview), it is necessary to change your microskill lead or interview plan based on this new data.

More details on active mastery may be found in Ivey's *Intentional Interviewing and Counseling* (1994).

## THE MILLIPEDE EFFECT

The specific and concrete approach to the interview in this book has been demonstrated to be effective. But at the same time, many students in the early stages find the method a bit awkward and uncomfortable. The story of the millipede below may be helpful to you as you test out your abilities with these skills and strategies.

An old fable tells about the fly and the millipede. It seems the millipede was walking along the road when a fly came buzzing by and landed. The fly looked the millipede over and marveled at the way the millipede could coordinate a thousand (or so it seemed) legs.

"Pray, millipede," said the fly, "how dost thou work all those many legs together so smoothly?"

"No sweat," said the millipede, "I just do it."

The fly flew away marveling at the coordination of the many-legged creature.

After the fly left, the millipede pondered the conversation. "Now just how do I move all those legs so marvelously? Do I do three left and three right and then alternate down the line, or perhaps it is one at a time?"

And as the millipede examined how he did it, he fell into the ditch.

*Moral: if you look too closely at how you do things you can get into trouble.*

And so it goes with microtraining. The single skills approach will at times be awkward and uncomfortable. You may find yourself troubled and uncoordinated. Missing from the old fable, however, is the fact that skill training—the analysis of what one is doing—eventually results in superior performance.

The basic analogy can be applied to tennis or ballet. One can play tennis or dance without knowing the systematic steps (grip, stroke and position, movement), but training in the component parts of tennis and ballet improves skill and enables one to achieve complete mastery. Polanyi speaks of *tacit knowing*. Through systematic, step-by-step training in tennis or ballet, one often goes through the millipede effect (i.e., natural movements at first become awkward due to changes imposed by instruction), but at some point in the future with *practice*, the new movement becomes smoother and more natural than it was originally.

## TEACHING SKILLS AND STRATEGIES TO OTHERS

The final chapter of this book presents teaching suggestions. The helper is gradually assuming a new and important role in society, that of direct teaching of helping and communication skills. You can work on a one-to-one basis through counseling and therapy and can be of assistance to a few people, or you can teach effective communication skills to many helpees and clients.

One specific strategy that is most useful is teaching clients individually or in small groups how to be effective communicators. One possible future role for you is to teach these skills to your helpees. Another is to train volunteer helpers or community workers with these skills. With that in mind, you may want to give special consideration to Chapter 9 which shows how to teach the skills you will be working with in this book. Think of teaching communication as one important strategy for helping.

The helper of the future will be a teacher—but a teacher with a difference. As you move through this series, learn the skills and think through the potential for a new role—that of teaching people how they can communicate more effectively and enjoyably with others. Helping and helping skills are too important to keep to ourselves.

## MULTICULTURAL IMPLICATIONS OF MICROTRAINING

Our clients vary in their cultural backgrounds—gender, ethnicity/race, affectional orientation, physical capacities, spiritual/religious background, and experience of trauma (e.g. Vietnam veterans and cancer survivors both represent special cultures because of unique circumstances). How valid are the skills and strategies for people of differing backgrounds?

African Americans, Asian Americans, European Americans, Latina/os, Native Americans, and many other ethnic/racial groups have gone through microskills training. In fact, the methods have been translated now into at least fourteen different languages throughout the world. The ideas presented here have been used in the training of feminist counselors, with the deaf and blind, and with conservative and liberal religious groups.

The general conclusion is that the concrete and specific approach of microskills is welcomed and endorsed by a wide array of people. At the same time, we must recall that the skills need to be adapted to meet individual and cultural differences. For example, direct eye contact is the European and European American norm. The same eye contact may be disrespectful from a traditional Native American framework, but appropriate if this individual is widely experienced in U.S. and Canadian culture.

In general, research finds that women across many cultures seem to be more oriented to listening skills than men. Men tend to ask more questions. Questions may be seen as rude and intrusive and inappropriate with some individuals and some cultural groups. Self-disclosure is generally suggested as a skill which should be used sparingly in theory, but if the client comes from a different background, the sharing of your own life experience may actually help form a bond of trust, particularly in the early stages.

In short, there are no hard-and-fast rules. If you have an open, pleasant manner and are competent, this goes a long way in generating a respectful co-constructive relationship with your helpee. Learning about individual, group, and cultural differences is a life-long experience.

If you and your client are from culturally different populations (e.g. African American and white European American, a male and a female, physically able and physically challenged), anticipate that bringing out the story may be more complex. Issues of trust and different life experience deeply affect how completely and honestly helpees are willing to share.

A broad rule when your life experience is different from your client is that you often need to do three things: 1) ask how the helpee feels about working with you as an African American, white, man, woman, or physically different person; 2) share some of your own life story or something about yourself briefly, but do not take the focus away from the helpee; and 3) perhaps most important, be authentically yourself and share warmth and caring openly—your ability to be a truly helping personality is likely your best asset. Always share with care.

## SUGGESTED REFERENCES

Ivey, A., Gluckstern Packard, N., & Ivey, M. (1993) *Basic Attending Skills*. Microtraining, An Imprint of Alexander Street Press, 3212 Duke Street, Alexandria, VA 22314.

This book and the accompanying videotape series is the foundation for *Basic Influencing Skills and Strategies*. Contact Microtraining Associates at the above address for information on research regarding the model and translations in other languages.

Evans, D., Hearn, M., Uhlemann, M., & Ivey, A. (2011) *Essential Interviewing: A Programmed Approach*. Belmont, CA: Brooks/Cole.

The concepts of *Basic Attending Skills* and *Basic Influencing Skills and Strategies* presented in programmed text format.

Gluckstern, N., Packard, R., & Wenner, K. (1980) *Conflict Prevention Skills for Corrections*. Microtraining: North Amherst, MA.

Designed for corrections situation, this book and tape series is useful for managing some difficult situations.

Ivey, A. (2010) *Intentional Interviewing and Counseling: Facilitating Development in a Multicultural Society*. Belmont, CA: Brooks/Cole.

Overview of the microskills and the interview. Special attention is given to multicultural issues and generating a systematic treatment plan.

---

Ivey, A. & Authier, J. (1978) *Microcounseling: Innovations in Interviewing, Counseling, Psychotherapy, and Psychoeducation.* CC Thomas: Springfield, Ill.

Currently under revision, this book contains the extensive data base of 150 studies completed on microcounseling at that time. At this point, some 300 studies have been completed examining the model.

Ivey, A., D'Andrea, M., & Ivey, M. (2012) *Counseling and Psychotherapy: A Multicultural Perspective.* Thousand Oaks, CA: Sage.

The major theories of counseling and therapy are presented with an emphasis on concrete skills which are useful in treatment in a gender and multiculturally aware interview.

Ivey, A. and Matthews, W. (1984) A meta-model for structuring the clinical interview. *Journal of Counseling and Development*, 63, 237–243.

The original article presenting the five-stage structure of the interview as presented in this book.

Pedersen, P. & Ivey, A. (1994) *Culture-Centered Counseling and Interviewing Skills.* New York: Greenwood.

Issues in culture and how to apply counseling skills in culturally varying situations.

*Special note:* A variety of videos oriented to multicultural and practice issues are available from Microtraining Associates, an imprint of Alexander Street Press. www.emicrotraining.com

# CHAPTER 2

## THE BASIC LISTENING SEQUENCE: SEARCHING FOR STRENGTHS AND SOLUTIONS IN THE HELPEE'S STORY

The first necessary element in effective helping is to *listen* to the helpee. Too many beginning (and some experienced) interviewers rush rapidly to find resolution to the helpee's concern. Most likely, the issues developed over a period of time. Before moving to problem resolution, take a moment and hear the story.

*Basic Influencing Skills* assumes you have some experience in listening skills. This chapter reviews the skills with a focus on helpee storytelling. In addition, we will introduce the importance of the positive asset search as it relates to solution-oriented counseling and therapy.

This chapter seeks to encourage you to:

1. Stop a moment and think of someone who listened to your story when you needed to be heard.

2. Read and review the skills of listening as organized in the basic listening sequence, Microskills Strategy #1.

3. Examine how Microskills Strategy #2, the positive asset search, can be used as a basis for resolution of issues and helpee concerns.

4. View a videotape or witness a live demonstration of these concepts in the interview.

5. Practice the basic listening sequence and positive asset search as you listen to a helpee's story.

6. Generalize the ideas of the two Microskills Strategies into real life settings.

## LISTENING AS THE FOUNDATION OF THE HELPING RELATIONSHIP

We all have had times in our lives which proved difficult and trying. Most of us have been fortunate to have someone *there* to be with us and hear our story. Take a moment and recall what it was like for you during one of these troublesome periods. Especially recall the emotions you felt around that story.

If you were lucky, that special person took time to listen and be with you. They heard your story. It may help to close your eyes and imagine the person who helped. Recall how they listened and remember your feelings as you were heard.

Use the following space to make some notes on your thoughts and feelings about this recollection.

_____

_____

_____

_____

_____

_____

Sometimes this exercise brings out negative recollections of when your story wasn't heard. If this occurs for you, make brief notes and think about what a more positive experience might have been. This book and microskills theory believes that we always need to emphasize positive strengths and personal assets in our interviews.

It is often helpful to share these images and stories of listening with others. These experiences form a foundation for the future of effective helping.

## THE BASIC LISTENING SEQUENCE (MICROSKILLS STRATEGY #1)

A client often comes into a helping session confused and disorganized. The facts of the situation may be presented unclearly. The feelings may be hidden or they may be so strong that nothing else matters. *The major task of listening is to help the client sort through the facts and the feelings, and to organize these facts and feelings into a meaningful pattern.*

Let us assume a client comes into an interview talking about the spouse's drinking. Your task is to draw out the facts, how the client feels about those facts, and to organize them. To learn about the client's problem, use the basic listening sequence.

1. *Open questions* to obtain a general picture of the situation.

   "Could you tell me how you view the problem?"

   "What is going on?"

   "How do you feel about the situation?"

   "Why do you think he/she is drinking?"

   "Could you give me a specific example of an argument you had?"

We would ask you to pay special attention to the last open question. This question asks for a specific example. You will find that some of your helpees talk rather abstractly about their issues. You will find that even one concrete, detailed example of a family conflict, a drinking situation, or other concern, will help you understand much more clearly what is occurring.

The helping profession calls this *concreteness.* And you will find that open questions are especially important in helping your client become more concrete and specific.

2. *Closed questions* to obtain some more facts and specifics.

"How old are you?"

"How old is your spouse?"

"How often do you argue?"

"Where?"

"How many children do you have?"

3. *Minimal encourages* to encourage further talk and elaboration on details. You will find that if you directly repeat exact words the client is saying in a questioning tone of voice, the client will then elaborate the meaning of the word or phrase in rather complete detail.
"Drinking *every* day before lunch?"

"Angry?"

"You say your children are having trouble in school?"

4. *Paraphrasing* to feed back the main facts of the situation as you have heard them.

"So you are saying that he/she drinks constantly, but it often happens after you have a fight."

"Your own background is from an alcoholic family and you have made the decision not to drink at all."

5. *Reflection of feeling* to feed back to the client the emotions underlying the situation.

"Sounds as if you feel *angry and hurt* much of the time, but still you have *feelings of deep caring.*"

"At this moment, you feel *discouraged*, but I also note you have had the *courage and strength* to face the situation directly and openly with me."

6. *Summarization* to organize the many facts and feelings of the person and situation.

"So far I've heard that you come from an alcoholic family yourself and you have deep feelings of anger and fear about alcohol. Your children are upset and doing poorly in school. Your spouse drinks early in the morning, but it seems worse after you have had a fight. Have I heard you correctly so far?"

You may have noted that these six listening or attending skills all seek to draw out the client's frame of reference concerning the problem. The spouse, the children, and you as interviewer may have another frame of reference. However, your task at this point is to understand the frame of reference of the client.

To understand a client's frame of reference, you need to know:

The *facts* of the situation. Obtain facts and details through open and closed questions oriented toward facts (particularly "what?" questions and, "Could you give me a specific example?").

Minimal encourages on key factual issues will draw out and elaborate information.

Paraphrase back to ensure that you have heard the facts correctly.

---

The *feelings* of the client. Obtain feelings through open questions oriented to feelings (especially, "How do you feel about that?") and reflection of feeling. The minimal encourage on feeling issues will encourage more in-depth understanding of emotion. Keep in mind that in most situations clients have several feelings toward other people and issues. This client, for example, undoubtedly feels love and anger, hurt and hope, and myriad mixed feelings. It is your task to help the client sort out the complex mixed facts and feelings.

The client's *organization* of the situation. This is done through the summarization skill.

Once the client's facts, feelings, and organization of a situation are clear, the specific avenues for further influencing skills may be clear. Sometimes, simple organization of facts and feelings may help the client come up with her or his own solution.

*Before you influence, listen to and learn the client's frame of reference (facts, feelings, and organization of thinking concerning an issue) through skilled use of the basic listening sequence.*

## POSITIVE ASSETS AND THE SEARCH FOR HELPEE STRENGTHS (MICROSKILLS STRATEGY #2)

Stories presented in the helping interview are often negative, full of problems and difficulties. People grow from strength, not from weakness. Carl Rogers, the founder of client-centered therapy, was always able to find something positive in the interview. He considered positive regard and respect for the helpee as essential for future growth.

The positive asset search is a more concrete way to approach positive regard and respect for the helpee. As you listen to the helpee, constantly search for strengths and positives. Then, feel free to share your observations. Of course, you do not want to become overly optimistic and deny the story the helpee is sharing with you. However, it is increasingly clear that if you only listen to the sad and negative parts of the helpee's story that progress and change will be slow and painful.

As a general rule, we suggest that you use the basic listening sequence to draw out the helpee's story in relatively brief form. Then repeat back and summarize the helpee's story to ensure that you have heard accurately. We are also recommending that you obtain at least one concrete specific example of the story to ensure mutual understanding.

As appropriate to the client and situation, begin your search for positive assets and strengths. If you develop with your helpee a list of strengths and assets, you will find you can draw on them later for resolution of concerns and problems. Naturally, do not push strengths against client wishes, as this may appear to minimize her or her concerns. However, seek to make a positive approach part of the interview and later treatment plan.

Some specific, concrete examples of how to engage in a positive asset search include the following:

Feedback—listen for strengths which the helpee may have, but is not stressing or may be missing as the story is told.

"As I listen to your story about the family drinking problem, I sense a lot of strength in the way you have been able to hang in there and still try to support your sister. Specifically, I heard the way you are able to take her out of the home, help her have fun on the playground, and just listen to her. That's a major strength you have."

Searching for times when the problem doesn't occur is often useful. With this information, you can determine what is being done right and encourage more of the same.

"Let's focus on the exceptions—when the problem or concern is absent or a little less difficult. Please give me an example of one of those times."

- "Few problems happen all the time. Tell me about a time when it didn't happen. That may give us an idea for a solution."

- "What is different about this example from the usual?"

- "How did the more positive result occur?"

- "What did he/she or you do or say when it went better?"

- "How is that different from the way you usually handle the concern?"

Personal strength inventory—helpees tend to talk about what they can't do. This puts them "off-balance." We can help them center and feel better about themselves through a strength inventory.

"As part of any interview, I like to do a strength inventory. Let's spend some time right now identifying some of the positive experiences and strengths you have which you have either now or in the past."

- "Could you tell me a story about a success you have had sometime in the past? I'd like to hear the concrete details."

- "Tell me about a time in the past when someone supported you and what they did."

- "What are some things you have been proud of in the past? Now?"

- "What do you do well or others say you do well?"

Cultural/gender/family strength inventory—here we move outside the individual and look at context for positive strengths.

- "Taking your ethnic/racial/spiritual history, can you identify some positive strengths, visual images, and experiences which you have had now or in the past?"

- "Can you recall a friend or family member of your own gender who represents some type of hero in the way they dealt with adversity? What did they do? Can you develop an image of them?"

- "We all have family strengths despite frequent family concerns. Family can include our extended family, our stepfamilies, and even those who have been special to us over time. For example, some people talk about a special teacher, a school custodian, an older person who was helpful. Tell me concretely about them and what they meant to you."

You obviously will not have time for all of the above. But, when we focus only on the negative story, we place our helpees in a very vulnerable position. They all have strengths. But it is vital that you do not become oblivious to concerns, issues, and problems. Again, do not use the positive asset search to cover up or hide basic issues.

Increasingly, the helping field is moving to awareness of the importance of giving some time to positives in each helping interview.

### VIEWING A VIDEOTAPE OR LIVE DEMONSTRATION OF THE POSITIVE ASSET SEARCH AND BASIC LISTENING SEQUENCE

Reading about skills and strategies is seldom sufficient. Microtraining has prepared videotapes illustrating these concepts, but live demonstrations in a group settings can be equally valuable. You may even want to develop your own videotape illustrating the concepts.

If your group uses a live demonstration instead of a prepared video, we suggest the following procedure:

- A volunteer helpee is selected who is willing to tell a story about a real or role-played concern. It is important that the volunteer let the helper know whether it is a real situation or not.

---

- A volunteer helper helps the helpee draw out the story by using listening skills.

- Observers—Use the space provided below to note the key facts of the helpee's story, the key emotions, and how the story is organized by the helpee.

After the story is completed and summarized to the helpee's satisfaction, the helper can then conduct a positive asset search using one or more of the specific strategies suggested in Microskills Strategy #2. The observers can summarize the positive assets.

Starting with the positive asset search (rather than always starting with the latest problem) will often help clients feel comfortable and take pride in themselves. Being grounded in the positive often enables helpees to examine difficult issues in more depth and with more hope.

Following is a listing of issues to watch for as you observe an interview. Make appropriate notes for reference and feedback.

Key Facts:

Key Emotions:

Organization of the Client's Story and/or Problem:

Positive Assets:

## PRACTICING THE BASIC LISTENING SEQUENCE AND POSITIVE ASSET SEARCH

You have now seen and read about these central concepts of listening. But what is most important is your ability to use them and demonstrate them in an interview. The following is suggested for a practical session:

1. *Develop a working group.* You can't practice alone. The most effective group size is three or four. However, two people can be sufficient for practice.

2. *Assign roles for the first practice session.* The following are listed in order of critical importance:

 a. *Helper.* This individual practices the concepts in a short role-play. The task is to draw out the narrative or story from the helpee and to learn the facts, feelings, and organization of the problem and asset. You will have achieved active mastery if you can bring out *the facts* of a client's concern, *the feelings* underlying those facts, and summarize with a systematic *organization* of what the client has been saying from his or her frame of reference. Specific listening skills have the following mastery associated with them:

 (1) Open questions lead to more client verbalization; "what" questions to facts; "how" questions to feelings; "why" questions to reasons; "could" questions to general exploration of an issue.

 (2) Closed questions lead to specifics and short verbalizations.

 (3) Encourages lead to more in-depth verbalization of the deeper meaning of the issue discussed, be it feelings, facts, etc.

 (4) Paraphrases lead to client verification of facts and thoughts.

 (5) Reflections of feelings lead to more discussion of feelings and verification of the feelings.

 (6) Summarizations lead to an organization of the client's facts and feelings.

(7) After you have brought out the helpee's story, spend some time with the positive asset search conducting a substantial inventory of helpee strengths.

b. *Helpee*. The helpee tells her or his story. After the role-play is completed, the helpee provides feedback for the helper.

c. *Observer/operator*. This person operates the videotape or audiotape equipment and provides verbal and written feedback to the helper. If no equipment is available, the emphasis is solely on observation.

d. *Second observer*. This individual provides written feedback to the helper and ideally concentrates observations on nonverbal dimensions which may be missed by others. This is especially important if no videotape is available for practice.

3. Determine topic for role-play. A very useful topic is personal experience with alcoholism. This can be a personal family story, or the reactions of the helpee to a friend or acquaintance. At issue is drawing out the story of an important concrete event involving alcohol. There are alternative topics such as a story of difficulty on the job, conflict with classmates or family, etc.

4. *Watch time carefully and provide feedback*. The role-play should be approximately five minutes and video or audio recorded. If not recorded, the observers become especially important to provide feedback. Use the feedback sheets provided and give specific information to the helpee. Do not be judgmental (e.g., "That was a great job!"). Rather, attempt to be specific and concrete (e.g., "You maintained eye contact appropriately and the client responded with a gradually relaxing body posture and vocal tone.").

5. *Rotate roles* so that every person has an opportunity to serve as helper and helpee. Again, remember to divide time equally. Be sure to obtain the facts, feelings, and organization of problem and assets.

---

**RATING SHEET FOR BASIC LISTENING SEQUENCE AND POSITIVE ASSET SEARCH**

Use the following form to classify skills of the helper. Note main words of the help-er's statement. You will find that using a form such as this makes it possible to reconstruct an interview with surprising precision.

Also, please circle the statements whose main words contain aspects of the positive asset search.

1. Were the facts, feelings, and organization of the client's problem and assets brought out (the critical active mastery level)?

2. Summarize what was learned in the positive asset search and how it might be useful in future interviews with this helpee.

| | MICROCOUNSELING SKILLS | | | | | | | |
|---|---|---|---|---|---|---|---|---|
| | Closed Question | Open Question | Min. Encourage | Paraphrase | Reflect. Feeling | Summarization | Other | |
| Helper Statement No. | | | | | | | | Main Words of Helper Statement |
| 1 | | | | | | | | |
| 2 | | | | | | | | |
| 3 | | | | | | | | |
| 4 | | | | | | | | |
| 5 | | | | | | | | |
| 6 | | | | | | | | |
| 7 | | | | | | | | |
| 8 | | | | | | | | |
| 9 | | | | | | | | |
| 10 | | | | | | | | |
| 11 | | | | | | | | |
| 12 | | | | | | | | |
| 13 | | | | | | | | |
| 14 | | | | | | | | |
| 15 | | | | | | | | |

(Continue on separate sheet as needed)

## GENERALIZATION

You have had an opportunity to review or learn the most basic concepts of microcounseling. If you have had prior experience in listening skill training, the concepts are familiar. What may be new is the objective—were you able to learn the facts, feeling, and organization of the client's concern?

It is this objective which we feel is most important in transfer of these skills. Research is clear that training such as this will be lost unless practiced outside of the training session and then regularly employed on a day-to-day basis. Thus we cannot emphasize too much the importance of using the skills immediately.

Here are a few generalizations we have found helpful in taking these skills beyond the book and training session. We suggest you review these with your trainer or teacher and contract to do one or more. With each skill in this book, we suggest you return here to look at possibilities for skill generalization and that you do "homework" with each unit.

1. *Use the skill in your daily life*. Make a contract with others in your group to take this skill home and use it with family and friends. Draw out the facts, feelings, and organization of family finances, a vacation trip, the building of an addition to the house. Note the facts, feelings, and organization of your child's behavior toward homework or friends. Talk to a friend about his or her vocational future and use the same skills.

2. *Practice on videotape or audiotape*. A brief practice session in a group clearly helps learning, but it is solidified if you buy an audiotape recorder and recruit a colleague or family member and *practice*. And practice for mastery—can you really draw out facts, feelings, and organization of a problem and an asset? Can you use all the microskills of listening? You may want to practice the attending skills of questioning, etc., one at a time for full mastery.

3. *Use the skill on the job*. If you are a salesperson, what are the facts, feelings, and organization of a client wanting to buy a car or a new suit? If you are a

secretary, what are the facts, feeling, and organization of your boss about the task just given you? If a manager, what are the facts, feelings, and organization of the problem on the production line? In counseling or interviewing practice, what are the facts, feelings, and organization of your client's problems?

4. *Teach the skill to someone else.* The final chapter of this book presents elementary microcounseling teaching procedures. Find one person (or a small group) and teach what you have learned to them. Measure your effectiveness using the feedback sheet there and note if your students are able to bring out facts, feelings, and organization when they talk with others.

5. *Make a typescript of your interviewing.* Before you start in-depth study of influencing skills, record an interview, make a typescript of it, and classify your helping leads. What positive assets do you see in your own natural helping style?

6. *Contract with one other person in your group to ensure that you do follow-up and use the skills.*

7. Finally, give special attention to the positive asset search in your daily life, in your interviewing practice sessions, at work, and in other settings. Note what occurs when you seek out the positive and take a more solution-oriented approach.

Write below your plan for ensuring that the skills are not lost, but are maintained. Important in this plan are your own facts, feelings, and organization of the material in this chapter. Is this material you can use? How?

# CHAPTER 3

# FOCUSING THE NARRATIVE:
# HELPING THE CLIENT SEE MULTIPLE PERSPECTIVES

Your first task usually is to encourage the client to tell the story. That alone may be enough. There is incredible power in sharing issues with a good listener. The organizing frame of the basic listening sequence sometimes provides a sufficient basis for the client to change behavior and act in new ways.

Listening may be described as a major influencing skill. Focusing the narrative or story is another way to help clients. The way you focus your listening helps shape how the helpee tells and understands the story. Used skillfully, focusing can enable the helpee to see the story in new ways, often very useful in the alleviation of concerns and problem resolution.

*Selective attention* is fundamental to the idea of focusing. *People tend to talk about things that other people will listen to.* For example, you may want to tell your friends about difficulties you just had with an exam or assignment or with a difficult relationship issue. Your friends may be more interested in their plans for the weekend and start talking about their concerns. They may start talking about their own problems with their relationship, ignoring your issues. Sometimes you find yourself listening to your friends when you really wanted them to listen to you.

There are also topics which many people avoid. One important example is an unsuccessful pregnancy in which the baby is lost. This is a story which needs to be told by the parents, for they have considerable hurt and pain to work through. An all-too-common pattern in our society is to avoid the pain of the personal story and say, "Well, it was all for the best—perhaps it was God's will." Very soon, many grief-stricken parents learn that their story is one which others don't want to hear.

Counseling and interviewing are interested first in focusing on the client's story from his or her perspective. In the negative examples above, note that the many listeners focus on their issues and ignore the concerns of the person in pain or wishing to explore a problem. The focusing strategies here are all aimed toward more complete examination of the helpee's life.

Finally, many agencies, community mental health centers, and schools are demanding more efficiency and accountability in interviewing and counseling. If you are aware of the concept of focus, you can help your client describe their issues more fully with less "wandering around."

This chapter asks you to:

1. Think about the way you selectively attend and listen to other people's stories. Do you listen from their frame of reference or do you change the focus to suit your own interests?

2. Read about the skills of focusing in Microskills Strategy #3 and consider how they may be useful for you.

3. View a videotape or live demonstration of the skill in practice.

4. Practice focusing so that it becomes more than an abstract idea. A skill which is clear in writing is not always so easy when it comes to actually using it.

5. Generalize the ideas of the focusing skills into real life settings.

## FOCUSING THE NARRATIVE (MICROSKILLS STRATEGY #3)

Imagine you are talking with a helpee and he or she starts to tell you a story about a difficulty in school.

> Client: I'm really uptight about the exam. The teacher doesn't seem fair to me. If I don't pass, my parents may cut off helping me. And, I can't get along with my roommate—she is so rich and snooty. The noise in the dorm is so bad I can't study. What am I going to do?

Write below how you might respond to this student if he or she were talking with you. What would you say next?

_____

_____

_____

_____

An analysis of the helpee's beginning story suggests many possible directions for focusing your response. Note that the italicized words below show how our language can affect what we might expect the helpee to say next. The italicized words are particularly important in changing focus, for they represent the "subject" of the sentence.

Helpee focus: "*You* feel frustrated and discouraged right now."

Helper focus: "*I* had a similar experience when *I* was in school and *I* know how difficult it can be."

Other individuals focus: "Tell me more about your *roommate*."

Problem or topic focus: "I hear several *issues and concerns*. Among them are the *exam* itself, your *roommate problem*, the *noise* in the dorm, *teacher and family pressure*, and perhaps *some others*. Which would you like to focus on first?"

Family focus: "Sounds like you feel like your *family* is threatening you. Tell me more about what's going on with them."

Cultural/environmental/context focus: "You said your roommate was *rich and snooty* and you have some *financial pressures*. Maybe we could talk a bit about how you feel about those *differences*?" (Starts the discussion around the cultural issue of social class.)

As you can see, client stories are often more complex than they seem at first. In such situations, the problem focus used above encourages the client to suggest the first direction for conversation and perhaps provides the helpee with the most choice and personal control. Missing from a problem focus, however, is how this unique individual client/helpee thinks and feels about the situation in school. Moreover, other foci above may be ultimately more important and you may wish to assist the helpee in exploring each.

It important to understand how you and your client's choice of focus affect how the story is told. To master the concepts of multidimensional foci, write alternative responses below. Each may facilitate increased understanding and enable the helpee to see new perspectives.

Client: I'm really confused. This guy just reached and fondled me. I thought he was really neat and we had such a good time on the first date, but it was gross. I didn't know what to do. He tells me that it was nothing and won't do it again. My parents are really conservative and if they knew, they would blame me for it even happening.

1. ***Helpee focus.*** Recall that the key words are the client's name and the words *you* and *your*. It often helps to personalize the interview if you use the helpee's name regularly. When we focus on the client, we hear the story from the helpee's perspective. Write a helping lead focusing on the helpee.

_____

_____

_____

2. *Helper focus.* This is also termed a self-disclosure and you share something of yourself. Self-disclosure of your own reactions and experience presents you with a difficult balancing act. If you share too much of yourself, you take away the stage from the helpee. If you don't share enough, you may lose trust and you may lose a valuable focusing strategy. Currently counseling theory is suggesting that modest self-disclosure and helper focus can be beneficial, but be sure to turn back the issue to the helpee immediately.

For example, "Does my sharing come close to yours at all?" "Is that near what you feel?"

Finally, with clients who are culturally different from you, helper focus and sharing of some personal life experience of you as a person may be beneficial in the early stages of helping. You will also find that feminist and women's theories of helping suggest the importance of sharing yourself early in the session, but always with the focus quickly returning to the helpee.

Write a helper self-disclosure focus and be sure to plan to pass the conversational ball back to the helpee.

_____

_____

_____

_____

3. *Other individuals focus.* An all-too-common problem with beginning helpers is to focus on other people not actually present in the interview. Watch yourself for that problem. If we focus on those not present, we let the helpee "off the hook" and often miss the story as the client would like to tell it. For example, a helpee may talk to you about a bad family experience. Many beginning helpers will focus totally on the family and forget to focus on the helpee sitting there before them.

However, full narratives and stories need the point of view of others. Asking the client, "How would your teacher/parents/friends/etc. talk about the situation?" and, "How would they tell the same story you just told me?" are two good ways to bring others into the conversation.

Write a question *and* a more listening, reflective response (paraphrase or reflection of feeling) focusing on other people involved in this situation.

_____

_____

_____

4. ***Problem, concern, issue, or topic focus.*** This orientation to focus is often central. Clients indeed do come to us to talk about their "problems." Thus, you will find that many of your helping leads focus here. A combination focus on both the individual and the issue, family and the problem, or cultural issues and the topic will enrich the discussion.

Write below one or more statements focusing specifically in this area.

_____

_____

_____

5. *Family focus*. The emphasis on family is new to this book. Family can be defined in many ways—traditional nuclear, extended, perhaps with the main caretaker being a grandmother, single parent, gay/lesbian, or even an important "family" put together in the form of close friends. It is important to encourage the client to present his or her own ideas of family. *Family of origin* is another important idea in the family focus. Here we look at how developmental history in the helpee's past may affect present life.

Our life stories are deeply affected by our past and present families. When possible, you will want to learn the perspective of family history and the present family as well.

Write below a question and a paraphrase/reflection of feeling around a family focus.

---

---

---

---

6. *Cultural/Environmental/Contextual Focus.* The environmental or situational context opens a wide array of possibilities. Counseling often seeks the solution in the individual whereas the situation or environment may be at fault. A woman or an African American's difficulties in coping with a campus environment may be caused by that same environment. Treating individuals when environments need change can be most ineffective. Write a CEC focus at the top of the next page.

_____

_____

_____

Focus may be *mixed*. A review of most of the examples in the preceding section will reveal that few of them are "pure" examples and, in truth, our conversation contains a wide mixture of foci and topics in any sentence. We would not advocate single focus comments, but use this method to help you become aware of the importance of focus within any interview.

## FOCUS AND PROBLEM ASSESSMENT

A simple, but logical extension of the focus concept is with elementary client assessment. It is important in assessing clients to consider all issues.

Let us assume a client comes in to discuss a retirement problem:

> Client: Five years into retirement! We didn't plan well enough. Our money is going due to inflation. What can we do?

Or perhaps a marital difficulty:

> Client: He just isn't interested in sex anymore. All he does is work. Just like his father. All talk, no action.

Focus analysis is useful in noting possibilities for directing and guiding the interview. It is also useful in providing an elementary framework for assessing the client's problem. In both examples above, you need to assess:

1. The *client* sitting there before you. Who is the client and how does she or he feel?

2. Yourself, the *helper*. What is your part? What are your parallel experiences, successes, blind spots?

3. *Others*. What about the absent spouse? Are there family members? Who are the key people involved?

4. The *problem*. What is the problem? What are some current assets?

5. The *family*. Many, or even most, of our concerns relate directly or indirectly to our family members. The way we think and feel about things often relates to our family history and present situation. The way we live now is most deeply affected by our family living situation. Missing family concerns when working with individuals can be a serious error.

6. The *cultural/environmental/context*. Should you be talking about the marital problem or about a society which produced divorce and inflation? What about sexism and ageism? What are the crucial situational variables involved?

In short, few problems are "simple." Most issues you will encounter touch all dimensions of focus. You will find it helpful as you start work with a new client to check out the several dimensions of focus. You might be tempted to start working on the problem immediately, but the real issue may be your relationship with the client or the larger situation or culture. Focusing provides an early, fairly complete and painless way to assess clients.

## VIEWING OF VIDEOTAPE OR LIVE DEMONSTRATION OF FOCUSING

While videos of the skill in action are useful, they are not always be necessary. You may wish to work with some others and make your own video or audiotape for a classroom demonstration.

How do you do this? First, select a topic and use the basic listening sequence to draw out the client's story. Then, deliberately go through each focus sequentially to ensure that each perspective on the client's original story is considered. You may even wish to have the specific pages of this book on your lap during the interview. In the early stages, referring to notes can provide a useful boost. Just be sure to share with your helpee what you are doing and why.

Then, watch the video or listen to the audiotape, write down a few words of each helper statement, and classify the focus.

## PRACTICING FOCUSING

1. Develop a working group of a pair, a triad, or four people.

2. Assign roles for the practice session.

    a. Helper. Your active mastery goal is to cover all focus dimensions and have the client discuss facts and feelings associated with each. Feel free to have them listed in your lap to ensure coverage. You may conduct a problem assessment.

    b. Client. Your task is to discuss one of the following suggested topics or another of your own choosing: an eating problem, reactions to a significant life experience (accident, death, marriage). You may wish to present a suitable issue for problem assessment such as vocational choice, a problem with a friend, or a financial planning issue.

    c. Observer/operator. Runs equipment and completes Focus of Conversation Scoring Form.

    d. Second Observer. Give special attention to concepts of active mastery. Does the client talk about facts and feelings associated with each focus?

3. Conduct five- to eight-minute practice session.

4. Provide feedback and watch time carefully.

5. Rotate roles as time permits.

## FOCUS OF INTERVIEW CLASSIFICATION FORM

Main Focus Words of Helper

| | Helpee | Helper | Others | Problem | Family | C/E/C |
|---|---|---|---|---|---|---|
| 1. | | | | | | |
| 2. | | | | | | |
| 3. | | | | | | |
| 4. | | | | | | |
| 5. | | | | | | |
| 6. | | | | | | |
| 7. | | | | | | |
| 8. | | | | | | |
| 9. | | | | | | |
| 10. | | | | | | |
| 11. | | | | | | |
| 12. | | | | | | |
| 13. | | | | | | |

---

## FOCUS ACTIVE MASTERY FEEDBACK

1. Was the helper able to use all foci in assisting the client to obtain a more comprehensive view of the issue?

2. Do you believe that any specific focus might have been stressed more? Less?

3. Was the helper able to bring out facts and feelings of each focus dimension? Note below those foci which were actually covered.

Helpee: _____    Helper: _____

Others: _____    Problem: _____

Family: _____    C/E/C: _____

4. What did each perspective add to completeness of understanding the story?

5. Other comments and feedback.

## GENERALIZATION

The practice session provided you with an opportunity to demonstrate that you can perform the concepts stressed in this manual. To generalize what you have experienced beyond this immediate session, complete one of the following two contracts, or write another of your own. Have a friend examine it for clarity.

1. An excellent way to work for generalization to daily life is to find a friend or family member who is willing and interested in exploring a concern or issue in more detail.

   First, use the basic listening sequence to draw out their story. Then, talk with them about the various foci and examine how the story was told the first time. Which foci did your friend or family member use most of the time?

Then, deliberately, with the volunteer helpee's awareness, focus the interview on each of the several possible foci. Make this a sharing experience in which the helpee is fully aware of how you are trying to enlarge and broaden the story from many perspectives.

Report back your degree of success with this approach. And, consider at times the possibility of doing exactly the same with real helpees. *It does not hurt at all to tell helpees what you are doing and why you are doing it.*

2. In a group situation during the coming week, I will spend 20 minutes noting the moving focus of the statements made by group members. Following this I will select a focus of interest to me and note my ability to influence the group to stay on this focus.

I will report back to the group my experiences.

Once again, *you don't know what you are doing until you can teach it to someone else.* Here is a suggested contract for teaching. Develop an alternative if you find it inappropriate.

I plan to teach one friend or family member in a 20-minute miniworkshop the ideas central to the concept of focus. We will then have a conversation and the individual I train will be given the responsibility of deliberately shifting focus. The measure of my effectiveness in teaching this skill to this individual will be measured by one of the following: 1) an audiotape recording which we score together; 2) a third person will watch the session and provide immediate feed-back on performance; or 3) we will stop after every third interchange and look back at the pattern of our focus change. Finally, we will spend five minutes talking about our mutual perceptions of the session, noting particularly where either of us distorted what we meant or what we heard.

# CHAPTER 4

# CONFRONTATION:
# SUPPORTING WHILE CHALLENGING

The effective helper meets and copes with situations directly and forthrightly. The ability to express oneself clearly—to "say what you mean and mean what you say," is central to any helping relationship. Confrontation—the accurate pointing out of discrepancies in an individual—is basic to many helping theories.

In this chapter, the usual format of microcounseling manuals and exercises will be presented. Specific competencies which are stressed in this chapter are:

1. Ability to identify discrepancies between what a person says and what is done, between people, or between people and situations.

2. Ability to identify confrontation statements as opposed to nonconfrontation.

3. Ability to feed back these discrepancies in a non-judgmental framework of reference through skillful confrontation.

Active mastery of confrontation skills is shown when clients are able to engage themselves in the contradiction posed for them and develop a new or more workable way to live with that contradiction or discrepancy. The client may resolve the discrepancy with a new, more encompassing thought pattern, work on a portion of the incongruity, or, perhaps, simply learn to live with an unresolvable contradiction. All of these levels of client reaction to a confrontation represent active mastery.

## GENTLENESS AND RESPECT—INDIVIDUAL AND CULTURAL DIFFERENCES

The very word *confrontation* implies conflict. *This is **not*** the meaning which confrontation holds for the helping interview. For whatever reason, confrontation is the word which the helping field has decided to use. Thus, it is important that we examine the meaning of confrontation in our field and contrast it with the usual use of the word.

You may prefer to think of confrontation as a "supportive challenge." Confrontation without empathy and understanding is empty.

Confrontation in interviewing is a positive way to help clients see themselves and their issues in new ways. We would add the word "gentle" and "respect" to the definition. In addition, confrontation needs to be presented in an open, non-judgmental fashion. The definition of confrontation in this text is as follows:

> Confrontation is gently and respectfully aiding helpees to look at themselves and the discrepancies and incongruities in their lives. The objective of a confrontation is to help the other person see things about their lives and situations which they may not have seen before.

> Gentleness and respect are essential foundations of any confrontation. With some clients, this demands that confrontation be subtle and more indirect. With other clients, a more direct and firm presentation of discrepancies may be necessary, but always with a gentle awareness of the uniqueness of each person and his or her individual and cultural background.

With a highly assertive, perhaps even aggressive client, you may feel at times that maintaining respect and gentleness is difficult, perhaps even irrelevant. Critical here is you being able first to listen carefully to the helpee, then to speak clearly and firmly, but always non-judgmentally and with respect. The absence of a negative judgment is itself gentle. You don't have to be soft to be gentle. Sometimes a very direct, forthright confrontation is necessary. Humor coupled with firmness may be useful with a person who wants to avoid looking at her or himself or may wish to avoid the truth.

On the other hand, some of the confrontation suggestions in this chapter would be considered rude and intrusive in some cultures. For example, a traditional Navajo or Asian American individual or family might prefer an even more respectful approach. Two possibilities for a more gentle approach to confrontation include:

1. Share some of your own stories (carefully) which may relate to the client's story. The story may be about your personal experience or a metaphoric story related in some way to the helpee's experience. Avoid being bookish or false. Metaphoric sharing has to be natural or it will be worse than a direct confrontation. Successful resolution of the discrepancy may at times be part of the story.

   With children you can often confront and help them take a new perspective by reading a relevant story from a children's book. Then compare their story with that presented in the book. "How do you handle difficulties with your friends?" "How did the hero in this book handle difficulties with friends?" "Is there anything you can learn from the hero?"

2. Another possibility is "incompleteness." You simply summarize the discrepancy and "leave it there." It will be heard and the helpee may wish to "work on it" in her or his own way.

Always think about respectfulness, gentleness, and maintaining a non-judgmental attitude.

## CONFRONTATION: (MICROSKILLS STRATEGY #4)

Confrontation is usually defined as a challenge and is often discussed as a conflict. A dictionary definition of confrontation is "to stand in the face of," "to face in hostility," "to oppose." Given this definition, it may be seen that many self-disclosure statements could be classified as confrontations (e.g., "I am going to stop you" is an expression of content; "I am outraged by that" is an expression of feeling). Clearly confrontations of this nature can either help or hurt. The effectiveness of these statements will depend on the context, the individual, and the specific timing of the intervention.

## CONFRONTATION

For purposes of this training manual, however, confrontation will be defined more narrowly as *the pointing out of discrepancies between or among attitudes, thoughts, or behaviors*. In a confrontation, individuals are faced directly with the fact that they may be saying other than that which they mean, or doing other than that which they say.

The advantage of this definition is that it is clear and has been demonstrated to have considerable value in helping oneself or another person look at a situation more realistically and accurately. The definition of confrontation focuses heavily on the fact that people are not always *congruent* and consistent.

Helpee confrontations ("you") might include:

"You say constantly that you are going to get up on time and get to work, but never do."

"You find yourself having mixed reactions to what I say. One side wants to agree, the other to fight and disagree."

"You keep saying you love your wife, but you constantly bicker and argue."

"Your words say you are comfortable talking about sex, but your lack of eye contact always comes when we talk about the topic."

Self-focused confrontations ("I") used by the helper might include:

"I, too, say I want to help myself stop smoking, but I just keep on."

"I think I intend to study, but I never start."

Dual-focused confrontations ("you" and "I") might include:

"Right now, *you* seem to be saying that *our* relationship has been good, but *my* experience—in this moment—is that *we* simply aren't communicating."

"On one hand, *you* say that I understand *you*, but, on the other hand, I feel puzzled and am not so sure that I do. *Let's* explore that some more."

The definition of confrontation presented above stresses the following factors:

1. A confrontation emphasizes discrepancies between or among attitudes, thoughts, or behaviors. "On one hand . . . , but on the other . . ."

2. A confrontation focuses on objective data. The more factual and observable a confrontation of discrepancies, the more helpful it may be. Confrontations are most effective when non-evaluative and non-judgmental.

3. Confrontations may be focused on self, the helpee, or any other of the several dimensions of "focus."

4. Any verbal statement may be scored as containing or not containing a confrontation.

5. Finally, a confrontation is not a blunt statement of opinion or emotion which disagrees with someone else. These are self-disclosure or feedback statements.

The objective nature of a confrontation—used appropriately with suitable timing—can be most helpful in aiding a client examine oneself or in helping people of varying opinions examine their differences.

The concepts of active mastery are useful in determining whether your confrontation is successful. You may give a perfectly good and appropriate confrontation, but if the client does not use it profitably, the confrontation has failed. The basic question is *what does your client do when encountered by your confrontation?*

*Consider the following as indicators of the impact of your confrontation. The higher on the scale, the more effective your confrontation.*

1. *Denial.* The individual may deny that an incongruity exists or fail to hear that it is there.

2. *Partial examination*. The client may work on part of the discrepancy.

3. *Full examination*. The client may engage the incongruity fairly completely, but make no resolution. It is here that active mastery is begun to be demonstrated.

4. *Decision to live with incongruity*. A confrontation may be successful if the person decides to accept the discrepancy as it is. Not all incongruities can be resolved. This itself is a higher level of client thinking.

5. *Development of new superordinate constructs, patterns, or behaviors*. A confrontation is most successful when the client recognizes the discrepancy, works on it, and generates new thought patterns or behaviors to cope with and perhaps change the incongruity.

## CONFRONTATION EXERCISES

Here is an interchange which provides an opportunity for a confrontation.

Helper:    Al, how are things going with Sue?

Helpee:    Well, things are going very well. I, you know, I don't mind the fact, the fact that she's gone all the time anymore. I think it's okay that she goes out and works evenings at the office. That, that, yeah, that's okay. I mean, it's really, it's really fine. The kids and I went out and saw a movie last night. Ah . . . and it was a good movie. So, it was okay. Yeah, I think things are going well. (All said in a flat monotone.)

Non-confrontations from the helper might include:

"Sounds like things are going better for you." (Paraphrase)

"What you say sounds phoney to me." (Ineffective feedback)

"I've had similar situations where things were hard at the beginning and later got better. For example . . ." (Self disclosure)

Confrontations might include:

"Al, you say that things are better, but your voice and expression suggest that perhaps it isn't there yet."

"On one hand, I hear you saying that things are better, yet my experience with you is different. On the other hand, I sense some confusion still."

Following are some helpee statements. Make confrontive and nonconfrontive responses to each.

1. Helpee: I'm making plenty of money. $8.00 an hour. Only problem is that I seem to spend it faster than I make it. For my age, that's good money. I think I know what I'm doing and can take care of it.

   Non-confrontive statement:_____

   _____

   Confrontive statement: _____

   _____

2. Helpee: My parents are getting along well. Oh, they argue now and then, but basically about minor things. They are really neat people, they never pressure me. I feel terribly guilty about not being able to get a job which they approve of.

   Non-confrontive statement: _____

   _____

**CONFRONTATION**

Confrontive statement: _____

_____

## VIEWING OF VIDEOTAPE MODELING DISCREPANCIES

You will see three videotapes or live demonstrations modeling at least three types of discrepancies. In the space provided, note the discrepancies and write a confrontation statement which catches the essence of the non-judgmental "On one hand . . . , but on the other. . . ."

1. Discrepancies between words and actions. "I don't know why you're on my case. I get my work in on time. Just because this report, just because this report is three weeks overdue." Note discrepancies here:

_____

What would a model confrontation sentence be?

"On one hand _____

_____

but on the other hand _____

_____."

2. Discrepancies among a person's emotions. "Wow I really feel torn. I've got this new job opportunity and it's really exciting, and it just shows a lot of promise and it's just exactly the people I'd like to work with. Sigh. But on the other

hand, there are just a lot of people here I like very much, and I've been very comfortable here. And making a decision between these two is really tough."

Note discrepancies here:

_____

What would a model confrontation sentence be? "On one hand you feel

_____ about _____

but on the other hand you feel _____

_____ "

3. Discrepancies between two people. "Well, my best friend and I got into this big argument. She says that I was flirting with her boyfriend. I mean, I never do stuff like that. It's not true at all." Note central discrepancies here:

_____

What would a model confrontation be? "On one hand, one person feels and

thinks _____

_____

but on the other hand, the other person feels and thinks _____

_____ "

## VIEWING OF VIDEOTAPE OR DEMONSTRATION MODELING CONFRONTATION

You may now find it helpful to watch an interview where discrepancies are confronted. Note, particularly, that many clients show a wide variety of incongruities or discrepancies in their behavior. In the first demonstration you will note that the counselor confronts too heavily and regularly even though the confrontations may indeed be accurate.

In the second session, you will observe that the interviewer uses the basic listening sequence and that skilled confrontation often results in clients finding their own resolution to the discrepancy. When clients are unable to provide their own resolutions, this is the time to use more direct influencing skills such as directives, self-disclosure, feedback, and interpretation/reframing.

Give special attention to active mastery concepts and use this space for notations on the confrontations you observe:

## PRACTICING CONFRONTATION

1. Develop a working group of a pair, triad, or four members.

2. Assign roles for the practice session.

a. Helper.

Your goal is to use listening and focusing skills to draw out the client's concern. While doing this, observe client discrepancies and provide confrontations.

b. Client.

Your choice of topic is particularly important. A topic or person on which you have mixed feelings is often appropriate. For example, most of us have mixed feelings toward our loved ones (parents, children, spouse). Developing a clarified awareness of these mixed feelings can be most helpful. Another good topic is a major difference of opinion between you and another person. Sorting out the two points of view may be a useful exercise for you as well as the counselor.

c. Observer I.

Complete the Confrontation Feedback Form.

d. Observer II.

Keep an ongoing log of interviewer statements on a separate piece of paper. You will not be able to keep a word-for-word log, but you will be able to provide enough for each counselor statement so that you can reconstruct the interview in your feedback session. Even if you have videotape or audiotape available, you will find that it is possible to obtain a better overview of the interview.

3. Conduct a five-minute practice session.

4. Provide feedback and watch time carefully.

5. Rotate roles as time permits.

---

**CONFRONTATION FEEDBACK FORM**

1. Discrepancies noted in the client (verbal or nonverbal):

2. Comments on the confrontational style of the interviewer. Was he or she able to maintain a factual, non-judgmental style? Was some form of the model sentence used, "On one hand . . . , but on the other hand . . . "?

3. Results of the confrontation in the client. What did the client do with the incongruity? (1. Denial; 2. Partial examination; 3. Full examination; 4. Decision to live with incongruity; 5. Development of a new superordinant construct, pattern, or behavior.)

## GENERALIZATION

Refer to the list of generalization items on pages 30–31 of the chapter on Basic Listening Skills. What specific action plan do you have to take these skills out and use them? Or what plans might you have to adapt the concepts to fit more easily into your own personal frame of reference?

# CHAPTER 5

# DIRECTIVES

## INTRODUCTION AND GOALS

We communicate to influence and to effect change. Directive-giving is the clearest example of some helpers' desire to influence others. The following is central in effective directives—*is what you want to happen clear and understandable to others?* Effective directives can result in immediate positive change.

For the teacher, the administrator, or the corrections officer, the importance of effective direction-giving is obvious. However, directives are also important tools of many professional helpers. One has only to look at a film or typescript of Perls, Ellis, or Wolpe to realize that directives play a significant role in the therapeutic process. Their directives are clear and to the point; their clients act on their directions. Equally important, these men communicate with their bodies, vocal tone, and eyes that they believe their directives are important and worth following. *The way that directives are given can be as important as the directions themselves*.

Marshall McLuhan has stated that the "media is the message." Effective direction-giving means not only giving clear directives, but you as the helper communicating that your message is worth receiving. Professional helping has given too little stress to the importance of interpersonal strength and competence in our work with clients.

The specific competencies sought in this workshop are below and the effective helper should be able to demonstrate them following training:

1. Define three basic dimensions of effective direction-giving.

2. Engage in the behaviors of effective direction-giving and demonstrate them on videotape and audiotape.

3. Identify and rate the direction-giving of others.

4. Use directives more effectively in your daily life and work.

5. Teach others how to give directives more effectively.

Active mastery of directives is indicated when your clients follow your instructions. Thus it is particularly important that careful attention be given to ethics and the clients' needs.

Further, you may wish to analyze the specific directives by well-known professional helpers and to determine if you wish to include their behaviors in your own repertoire.

## GETTING STARTED

What is your present ability to give directives? Do you like to give directions? Or is it something you avoid? Not all helpers want to give directions. You will have to decide whether or not you wish to give directives and how able you are in this skill.

As a first step, select a topic and give someone else or a small group directions. Possible topics include how to take a test, behave in a stressful interview, how to behave in a social situation, deal with a difficult coworker, or teach the basic listening sequence. Note below your feelings about giving directives and add to this feedback from those to whom you gave directives. Do you have any ideas about how you feel about directives at this point?

_____

_____

_____

_____

## DIRECTIVES: PUTTING YOUR IDEAS ACROSS (MICROSKILLS STRATEGY #5)

Three dimensions of effective direction-giving are stressed in this manual: 1) appropriate verbal and nonverbal behavior to support the directive; 2) concrete, clear directives; and 3) checking out with your helpee whether or not the directives were heard.

As a first step, however, directives should be defined. Some examples of verbal directives which might appear in a helping session include:

"Sit back in your chair, close your eyes, relax."

"Repeat what you just said, then repeat it again."

"After you leave here, count the number of times you find yourself putting yourself down to your friends."

"Have your right hand talk to your left hand."

"I want you to take a test."

The first dimension of effective direction-giving is appropriate verbal and nonverbal self-expressive behavior to support the directive. Physicians often talk about the "white coat" effect; if the physician appears to know what is being talked about, the patient will be more inclined to follow instructions. Similarly, the most able direction-givers of the helping profession have effective self-expressive behaviors of eye contact, vocal tone, and body language. Compare the effective helper with the weak or indecisive behavior of the parent or teacher who isn't quite sure what to do next to get the child or class to perform a certain activity.

A second dimension of effective direction-giving is *concreteness* or clear verbal specificity. The more clear and direct the statement, the more likely that directive is to be heard. Compare:

"You try that again." vs. "The first time you were looking at your hands. Say it again and look at me this time."

"Don't do that!" vs. "One of our agreed-on rules in this group is to talk one at a time. Okay, let's start with Sue."

"Tell me more." vs. "You just said you had a scary dream, then you wandered off to a discussion of dreams in general. Give me some specific things that happened in the dream that frightened you."

Further, when a series of directives must be given, it is more effective to give them *one at a time*, breaking them down step by step. For example, in teaching a microtraining session, don't give all the instructions for a group activity at once. First have the group break into small groups, *then* give the instructions. Later give additional instructions.

This leads to the third dimension or effective direction-giving, the "*check-out*." Check out with your group or individual whether or not your directives were understood. Ask your helpee(s) to restate the direction. Or, ask if your directives were understood. Allow sufficient time to make sure your ideas were followed. The beginning direction-giver often rushes at this point.

Specific examples of the check-out include:

"Could you tell me what I just said?"

"Are the directions clear? Do I need to say them again?"

"How does that suggestion come across to you?"

The first represents an open question seeking restatement, the second is a closed question allowing less participation, the third perhaps maximizes opportunity for the other to react to what you just said. To sum up basic concepts of direction-giving:

1. Use effective self-expression skills so you will be believable.

2. Be concrete and specific. One direction at a time is usually enough.

3. Check-out to see if your directives were heard.

## DIRECTIVES IN ALTERNATIVE THEORETICAL ORIENTATIONS (MICROCOUNSELING MANUAL #5A)

Directives are common in helping relationships. Overused, they take away client choice and freedom. Used judiciously, they provide the client with new options for considering her or his situation. Ethics and careful attention to client needs and wishes are critical.

Listed below are 17 different types of directives (they are by no means a complete list). You will find that some people respond to one type of directive, and others to different directives, and some will object to the directive style.

An open, receptive client may well respond to directives by acting immediately on your specific suggestions. A client who tends to be counter to authority (i.e., "counter-dependent") may respond most effectively to a paradoxical directive. Research and experimentation over the next several years may be anticipated to produce some conclusions as to which directive is most appropriate for which individual under what situation.

For the moment, however, it is suggested that you become skilled in more than one set of directives. You will find that a directive which doesn't appeal to you personally may be just what your client needs to start moving toward action or more interpersonal openness.

## EXAMPLE DIRECTIVES USED BY COUNSELORS OF DIFFERING THEORETICAL ORIENTATIONS

1. *Specific*          "I suggest you try . . . "
   *suggestions/*
   *instructions*
   *for action*

| | |
|---|---|
| 2. *Paradoxical instructions* | "Continue what you are doing . . . "<br>"Do the problem behavior/thinking/action at least three times." |
| 3. *Imagery* | "Imagine you are back in the situation. Close your eyes and describe it precisely. What do you see, hear, feel?"<br>"Describe your ideal day, job, life partner."<br>"Imagine you are going on a trip into your body . . . " |
| 4. *Role-play enactment* | "Now, return to that situation and let's play it out."<br>"Let's role-play it out again, only change the one piece of behavior we agreed to." |
| 5. *Gestalt hotseat* | "Talk to your parent as if he or she were sitting in that chair. Now go to that chair and answer as your parent would." |
| 6. *Gestalt nonverbal* | "I note that one of your hands is in a fist, your other is open. Have the two hands talk to each other." |
| 7. *Free association psychodynamic* | "Take that feeling and free associate back to an early childhood experience . . . "<br>" . . . to what is occurring *now* in your daily life."<br>"Stay with that feeling, magnify it. Now what flashed into your mind first?" |
| 8. *Reframing* | "Identify a negative experience, thought, feeling. Now identify something positive in that experience and focus on that dimension. Synthesize it with the problem." |
| 9. *Relaxation* | "Close your eyes and drift."<br>"Tighten your forearm, very tight. Now let it go." |

| | |
|---|---|
| 10. *Systematic desensitization* | a. Deep muscle relaxation. |
| | b. Construction of anxiety hierarchy. |
| | c. Matching objects of anxiety with relaxation. |
| 11. *Language change* | "Change 'should' to 'want to'." |
| | "Change 'can't' to 'won't'." |
| | Any new word/construct addition. |
| 12. *Staying with feeling/ emotional flooding* | "Go back to that feeling, get with it, make it totally you." |
| 13. *Meditation* | "Be still. Focus on one point. Relax. Concentrate on breathing. Let all thoughts slip from your mind." |
| 14. *Hypnotic trance* | "Fixate on that point. Relax. Note your breathing. Focus your awareness . . . " |
| 15. *Group work* | "Now I want you to do this . . . " |
| 16. *Teaching/ homework* | "Practice this exercise next week and report on it in the next interview." |
| | "Turn to page . . . " |
| | "Take out a sheet of paper . . . " |
| | "Take this vocational test . . . " |
| 17. *Family therapy communications* | "Don't talk to me . . . talk to him *now.*" |
| | "Change chairs with your wife and sit closer to your daughter . . . " |

From: *Intentional Interviewing and Counseling,* by Allen E. Ivey.
Copyright © 1994 by Wadsworth, Inc. Reprinted by permission of Brooks/Cole Publishing Company, Monterey, California.

## VIEWING OF DIRECTIVE DEMONSTRATION

The videotape supporting this skill area presents the interviewer briefly drawing out information from a client who procrastinates. This is followed by several alternative directives illustrating different theoretical orientations. Note how each directive is responded to by this client. Client response, of course, is the indication of active mastery. Alternatively, you may observe a live demonstration of relaxation training, imagery, or some other directive. Note that while helping is based on listening, at times taking direct action to aid the learning of new ways of thinking and behaving can be most useful. As you watch the demonstration, you may want to take note of these key points:

1. What were the facts, feelings, and organization of the client's concern about procrastination? Did the interviewer obtain a specific example?

2. What specific directives were used and how did the client respond to each?

## PRACTICING DIRECTIVES

1. Develop a working group.

2. Assign roles:

    a. Helper.        Your goal is as follows: 1) draw out the facts, feelings, and organization of the client's procrastination problem; 2) provide three alternative directives—but after each check-out how it was received and work some time with each before moving to the next.

    b. Client.        Most of us have procrastinated or delayed completing a task. The interview will be most effective if you talk about a current problem, but a past problem will be useful as well.

    c. Observer(s)    Provide feedback using the suggestions provided. One observer should keep a log of the helper's statements, writing down as many words as possible. This will make possible a fairly accurate recapitulation of the dialogue.

3. Practice, provide feedback, and rotate roles so all participate. For active mastery, an effective, clear and concrete directive leads to the client doing what he or she is directed to do. Does the client use the directive? Does it help?

---

## DIRECTIVES SCORING FORM

Giving directives involves four major emphases:

1. Demonstrating effective and believable self-expressive behaviors.

Scoring:    Score "+" if you personally find the eye contact, body language, words used, and vocal tone appropriate, "–" if you don't. This is a subjective judgment, but specific criteria derived from attending behavior can be used.

2. Giving specific rather than vague directives—concreteness.

Scoring:    Score "V" for vague if the directives are unclear and ambiguous. Score "C" (concrete) if the directives are clear and unambiguous.

3. Checking out to see whether the individual or group understands what is to be done.

Scoring:    The check-out can be explicit and is usually seen in verbal statements such as, "Do you understand?" or, "Repeat back to me what needs to be done."

However, implicit check-outs also appear in terms of a raised tone of voice at the end of a sentence, gestures, or patterns of eye contact. Score "+" for check-out, score "0" when absent or not needed, score "-" only when lack of a check-out or a poor check-out confuses the issue.

4. Active mastery: Does the client respond to the directive and do something? What? How effective was the directive?

Scoring:    Score "+" for positive impact and "-" for poor directives and/or non-compliance by the client.

| Directive | Self-Expressive Behavior | Concreteness | Check-out | Active Mastery |
|---|---|---|---|---|
| 1 | | | | |
| 2 | | | | |
| 3 | | | | |
| 4 | | | | |
| 5 | | | | |
| 6 | | | | |

## GENERALIZATION

I agree to use the skill of directions in the following situation:

_____

_____

Imagine that you are to teach a workshop to a selected group on the concept of directions. What steps would you use? What concepts would you emphasize? How would you give directions to your group? Develop a model workshop design now. Remember that one very important skill in running a microtraining session is the ability to give clear, concrete directives.

# CHAPTER 6

## FEEDBACK AND SELF-DISCLOSURE:
## TOWARD DEEPER COMMUNICATION IN THE INTERVIEW

Two related skills are emphasized in this chapter. The first is concerned with providing accurate and useful feedback to the client about how he or she is viewed by others. The second, self-disclosure, focuses on the sharing of your own personal perceptions and experiences with the client. Used separately or jointly, these two skills can do much to personalize the interview.

Feedback is most often associated with humanistic orientations to helping. However, direct, accurate feedback is useful in behavioral counseling, management performance appraisal, and in many other diverse settings. Self-disclosure, also, can be used in many different orientations to helping, *but* self-disclosure most importantly must be natural to your own style of being and to the present life situation of the client or other person. The central competencies to strive for in this chapter include:

1. The ability to draw out the facts, feelings, and organization of a client's problem.

2. The ability to provide relevant and timely self-disclosure to a client, enabling him or her to explore an issue in more depth.

3. The ability to provide accurate feedback to a client about how you see the client performing either in daily life or in the interview with you.

Active mastery of these skills is illustrated when your client talks in more depth or uses information to develop a new thought pattern or behavior, much as might be the result of a successful confrontation or directive.

## INDIVIDUAL AND CULTURAL ISSUES

Feedback and self-disclosure place you and the helpee in a more equal relationship. They demand that you be authentic, appropriate, and keenly attuned to where the helpee "is at." Used ineffectively, these skills can be disastrous.

A negative example first—and sadly, it is real. The helpee is a young person who has to make a formal presentation to a small business group for the first time. The helper is older and experienced in large group presentations.

Helpee: I have to make the presentation on the new product to all five members of our department tomorrow. It makes me really nervous.

Helper: I can understand. I make lots of presentations. I used to get nervous when I spoke to large groups of up to 300. Now I'm used to it. You'll be able to do it!

The above is not likely to be reassuring to the helpee. The helper is authentic and genuine, but clearly out of touch. Be sure your experience is within the past experience of the client or you may disturb the helping relationship more than help it by your self-disclosures or feedback.

Cultural background makes self-disclosure complex. If you are culturally different from your helpee, it often helps to discuss this issue "up front" in a honest manner by asking the helpee how he or she feels working with you. This has to be done with sensitivity.

Feminist counseling theory suggests that an equal relationship between helpee and helper is vital as a long-term goal. The gradual increase of mutual self-disclosure may be considered appropriate so long as the helper does not take over from the helpee. On the other hand, if you have a vulnerable or troubled client, sharing on your part may be inappropriate.

It is also important to recall that clients in severe distress may prefer that you work in a more hierarchical manner. They may feel more comfortable with you making the early decisions as to what they should or could do. Use your power carefully and aim later to move toward a more equal relationship in the helping process. Some traditional clients will prefer a more "professional" and hierarchical approach as well.

In summary, if you engage in the skills of feedback and self-disclosure, *attune yourself to the client's world.*

## FEEDBACK AND SELF-DISCLOSURE

*Feedback* may be defined as clients being told how someone else sees them and their actions.

*Self-disclosure* may be defined as the sharing of personal data and experience.

If you tell someone how you (or others) feel and think about them, you are giving feedback. If you share your own present and past experiences you are being self-disclosing. The two skills are obviously closely related and often overlap. The major difference is a focus on yourself (self-disclosure) and a focus on the other person or client (feedback).

Some questions to prompt thinking about your past experiences with feedback and self-disclosure follow. Record some of your thoughts below.

1. Most of us have had some unpleasant experiences with feedback from our boss, a friend, or family member. While it might be painful, think back on those experiences and specify what the person did which made the experience painful. What specifically did they say? How did they say it? In what situation?

2. Think of a positive experience in which "seeing oneself as others see you" was helpful and perhaps produced positive change or growth on your part. What specifically did the person say? How did they say it? In what situation?

_____

_____

_____

_____

_____

3. Self-disclosure can be overused or embarrassing. Can you think of a time where someone talked so much about themselves that you couldn't get a word in about your problem or experience? Sometime when a person revealed too much and embarrassed you and others? Perhaps when someone said, "When I was your age, I . . ."

4. Positive self-disclosure can help a person learn how others have experienced the same event. We can learn from others' perception of the world. How has someone else sharing their experience, feelings, and ideas been helpful to you?

## FEEDBACK (MICROSKILLS STRATEGY #6)

To see ourselves as others see us,
To hear ourselves as others hear us,
And to be touched as we touch others
These are the goals of effective feedback.

Whether we believe it or not, we have an impact on the world. When we talk to a clerk in a store, our tone of voice, body language, and actions touch that clerk for a moment. On the job, our work impacts others whether we do a good job or a poor one. Our personal actions and feelings affect our friends and family. Even if we do nothing (for example, we might fail to correct a child's behavior or forget to visit a sick friend), we have impact.

What is the nature of our impact on the world? The best avenue toward learning one's impact on the world is *feedback* from others. When we learn how we "are coming across," we discover we are having more impact than we believed and we can use those data for future actions.

*Feedback may be defined as providing accurate data on how the counselor or others view the client. It facilitates client self-exploration and self-examination. It can change behavior. If overused, particularly in a destructive fashion, it can destroy the client's self-concept and feelings of worth. It is a powerful and important skill.*

How can you give effective feedback? Here are some principles which may be helpful:

1. *Be concrete and specific* as opposed to being vague and general.
   "You're coming across in a nasty fashion." (Vague and general)
   "You appear angry because of your furrowed eyebrows and tense body. Your words come out very fast." (Concrete and specific)

2. *Be non-judgmental* as opposed to judging the client.
   "Looking so cross is a bad thing to do." (Usually judgmental feedback includes a good/bad judgment.)
   "Your tense face appears to me as anger. Is that what's going on with you?" (Non-judgmental. Note that it gives the client room to explore.)

3. *Focus on strengths* as opposed to weaknesses.
   "Looking like that must feel very miserable." (Weakness)
   "The tenseness and impression of anger seems to indicate that you are trying very hard." (The search for the positive asset may be critical. Too much feedback focuses on the negative.)

4. *Emphasize facts* rather than impressions; avoid labels. Impressions may be used, but allow room for client reaction.

"Your report is lousy." (Impression)

"Your report is two days late and contained many typing errors." (Facts)

"Your report appears ill-prepared. Could you tell me about what happened and your views on the report?" (Impression with room)

5. *Check-out to see how the feedback was received* rather than leaving it there by itself.

"You come across tense and angry. Is that the way you feel?"

"You give the impression of trying very hard. Is that accurate?"

"The report was late, contained some errors, and gave the impression of a rush job. How do you react to that? I'd like to hear your point of view."

In summary, note the "1-2-3" pattern of:

1. Observing the client using observation and listening skills.

2. Provide lean, accurate, and specific feedback.

3. Check out the impact of what you have said to determine how useful the feedback was and whether or not the client heard you.

## SELF-DISCLOSURE (MICROSKILLS STRATEGY #7)

How much should you share yourself with the client? Effective sharing of you and your personal experiences can facilitate a client's growth and self-exploration. Ineffective self-disclosure can cause awkward pauses and stop the client from talking.

Important in self-disclosure are the following:

1. *Genuineness.* Is it a real experience or thought or feeling you want to share about yourself? The self-disclosure must be natural and a part of you. If you have thought carefully about exactly the right thing to say, it still may be the right thing, but lack the genuineness which truly makes it received by the client.

2. *Relevance and relationship*. If the client is talking about a difficulty of getting along with a partner, it does little good for you to share a problem you have in getting along with one of your students in a class. However, brief sharing of a related problem you had with your own partner may indeed be helpful. Does the self-disclosure assist the relationship?

3. *Present or past tense*. If you want to move the interview more quickly and develop a strong relationship between you and your client, a present tense self-disclosure (e.g., "Right now, I sense your pain and hurt.") may help. In other situations, a change of tense and emphasis may be helpful (e.g., "I sense your feelings of caring . . . it reminds me of my own feelings toward my partner . . . ").

Generally, the most powerful self-disclosures are present tense and refer to the client (and may closely resemble feedback)— "Right now, I feel moved by your experience . . . I care where you are and what happens to you." However, used inappropriately, this self-disclosure could destroy your relationship.

4. *Checking-out*. Again, finding out how the client responds to your self-disclosure may be helpful. "How does that come across?" "Is that close?" "Any reactions to what I said?" The "1-2-3 pattern" of attend, self-disclose, and check-out is useful.

Self-disclosures can only be tested in the relationship of the interview. What appears to be a very bad self-disclosure may be surprisingly effective given the right situation. What technically is an excellent self-disclosure may be destructive. The usefulness of your self-disclosure can only be determined by your client's reaction. Thus the importance, again, of checking out how you were received.

## VIEWING OF VIDEOTAPE OR DEMONSTRATION SESSION

In this demonstration you will see the following steps designed to illustrate how feedback and self-disclosure might be used in an interview. Use the space to make notes.

1. The basic listening sequence to draw out the client's concern.

2. Use of self-disclosure to present a parallel experience.

3. Use of feedback to indicate to the client how he or she is coming across.

4. Active mastery. How did the client respond to these skills?

## PRACTICING FEEDBACK AND SELF-DISCLOSURE

1. Develop a working group for practice.

2. Assign roles for the practice session and plan for the interview.

*Client.* Present a problem you have had with peer or family pressure, eating, working too hard or not hard enough, or another concern.

*Helper.* Draw out that concern, using the basic listening sequence. Once you have an organization of the client's facts and feelings about that situation, self-disclose a parallel experience of your own. Then, be sure to check-out with the client how he or she reacted to your self-disclosure.

# FEEDBACK AND SELF-DISCLOSURE

After you have checked out the self-disclosure and listened further to the client, provide the client with feedback about how you see the client coming across in this issue.

*Observer/operator*. Record the interview and provide feedback, using the feedback and self-disclosure form. Keep a log of all helper statements so you can reconstruct the session.

3. Five minute role-play followed by feedback and discussion. Rotate roles. Provide data on active mastery.

## FEEDBACK AND SELF-DISCLOSURE FEEDBACK SHEET

1. Was the interviewer able to bring out the facts, feelings, and organization of the client's concern? What were some strengths you observed?

2. What was the nature of the interviewer's self-disclosure statement(s)? Genuine?

Relevant to this relationship? Present tense or past tense? Was a check-out used?

3. How effective was the interviewer's feedback?
   Concrete and specific?

Non-judgmental?

Some focus on strengths?

---

Emphasize facts rather than impressions?

Check-out included?

4. Active mastery. What was the impact of the interview on the client?

## GENERALIZATION PLAN

Write below your specific plans for taking this skill out of the training session, adapting it to your specific style.

# CHAPTER 7

# INTERPRETATION/REFRAMING:

# CHANGING THE MEANING OF THE STORY

Perhaps the most mystical and powerful helping skill is that of interpretation. One imagines the psychoanalyst delving deep into the psyche and with one brilliant stroke defining the essence of the patient's innermost problems. Analysts, psychotherapists, and counselors give special attention and prime study to accurate interpretation . . . and generally the "deeper" the interpretation, the more effective and meaningful it is thought to be.

Our approach to interpretation is, as you might expect, somewhat different—but, we feel, no less important, no less powerful.

*Interpretation is defined as the act of reframing or redefining "reality" (feelings, attitudes, behavior, situation) from a new point of view.* In short, there are a multiple number of interpretations possible to describe anyone person, group, organization, or even culture. The more interpretations one has available, the freer one is to be of assistance and the more opportunity for "understanding" to develop.

Narrative therapy is an important approach in the helping field. Essentially, what narrative therapy does is facilitate helpees in talking about or reframing their life stories in new, more positive ways. The basics of an entire theory of helping rest on the major assumptions and beliefs of this chapter.

> *To reframe a problem or concern is to change the nature of the issue. To rename or reframe a life story may be enough to change a life.*

We do believe that helping others talk about their lives in new ways can make an immense difference. You will find that the skills taught in this chapter will be useful both for yourself and for others. The abilities emphasized are:

1. Ability to define and rate interpretations.

2. Ability to generate a wide variety of alternative interpretations of life experience.

3. Ability to enable a helpee to interpret his or her own world with a variety of alternative statements.

4. Ability to use interpretation to help a client reframe past negative experiences more positively.

5. Ability to help others tell their life stories and to think about them in new ways.

## INTERPRETATION AND CREATIVITY

The roots of interpretation lie in creativity, the ability to make something new from what already exists. Creativity demands that one be able to view things from a new and different perspective, that one be able to assemble existing pieces into new wholes, and that one be able to take things apart and reconstruct a new picture—perhaps more complete and descriptive than existed before.

Consider the following . . . how many squares do you see in the figure below?

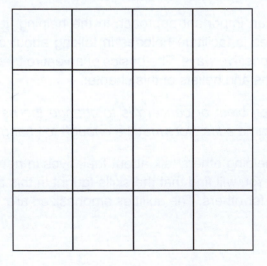

Most people say 16 at first glance. Then, recognizing the large square surrounding the figure, they say 17. Through a variety of *alternative ways of perceiving* the figure, it is possible to define 30 squares. Or perhaps you found even more?

This figure can be used as a basic analogy to interpretation. Most people see reality "as it is" when they first look at a situation, person, or object. It is difficult to "break set" and "come at" a situation in a new way once that first picture is developed. Creativity training can help prepare you for interpretation and develop readiness and ability to find the alternative points of view necessary for successful interpretation. Those who can develop a more creative approach to life tend to be those who are most able to innovate creative interpretations of life experience.

Try some of the following creativity exercises.

• Look about the room. Become aware of colors, then select one color and notice how light and shadow interact with that color. Notice shapes . . . squares and circles. Close your eyes and note sounds. Take an object in the room and touch it with your eyes closed, then open, noting texture and shape. Concentrate on odors. Notice people . . . how are they the same? Different? How many categories of people can you generate? Become aware of hands, noses. Imagine that the group has shape, texture; notice shading of colors in the skin. Your environment is an exquisitely rich source of stimulation if you will begin to explore it. Basic to creativity is noticing and being aware of what "is."

• Can you cut a pie into eight pieces using only three cuts? If so, how many ways can you do it?

• Imagine that someone has given you 1,000,000 plastic straws. What can you do with them?

• Look at some spot in the room different from where you are now. Imagine what the view will be from there and then go there. Notice what appeared as you expected it would . . . and what is different.

- Instead of 2 + 2 = 4, ask yourself the question, how many ways could you use numbers and end up with the answer 4?

- Columbus arrived in the "New World" in 1492. How many different views of the meaning of his arrival can you generate?

## INTERPRETATION: A MORE PRECISE DEFINITION

The purpose of this description is threefold: 1) to examine the concept of interpretation in relation to how differing psychological theories and/or *frames of reference* may lead to vastly differing renamings of the same situation; 2) to examine the "depth" of an interpretation; and 3) to compare interpretation with attending and other influencing skills.

1. *Reframing and the concept of frame of reference:*

Interpretations vary with the world view, theory, and frame of reference of the person presenting the reframing or new label. Depth interpretation, in particular, depends on theoretical "unseen" constructs. The Freudian frame of reference requires one to search for "oral," "anal," and "phallic" implications and may result in discussions of "dependency," "power," and "sexuality." In this case, the broad frame of reference is analytic psychology, the specific names are orality and dependency, anal behavior and power, and phallic-genital and sexuality.

*The frame of reference—the world view—of the psychological theory provides a grouping of names and labels.*

Imagine a person who works hard at the factory or office, seeks considerable overtime, and seldom takes a vacation. Various psychological theories might name this person very differently and recommend varying types of treatment. Stop for just a moment: When you hear of this type of person, how do you think about and name this type of behavior?

1. The psychoanalytically-oriented helper might see this behavior as representing a need for power and control, perhaps stemming from past difficulties with parents. The suggestion might be for long-term treatment.

2. The cognitive-behavioral counselor might name the business person as over-stressed and recommend relaxation training and other stress management procedures.

3. An employment counselor working with the company might see this person as an ideal employee, one ready for promotion.

4. The unemployed might name the person as "lucky to have a job." If the factory went on strike, they may support the worker during that time or they might seek to get the job themselves and serve as "strikebreakers."

Theory and our personal experience help us interpret and make meaning of the events in our lives. The facts of the busy worker remain the same, but the way we frame or interpret "reality" can be very important. Contrast your meaning-making of the business person with that of the four other approaches presented here.

Each of the meanings above, however, comes from external sources. As counselors, interviewers, and helpers, our task is to help the client interpret and make sense of the world.

The essence of this preliminary discussion of interpretation/reframing is that how we name or interpret life events can be very important. The frame or glasses through which we view events or behavior are at times as important as what we see or hear. As we seek to help others, we first need to clear our glasses and hold back on theory—and after we have listened, we share a new point of view.

Interpretation and reframing are presented here as a new point of view, a new way of looking at things, a new set of names—any of which may help the client feel better about self and enabled to take new action.

2. *Interpretation as reframing the narrative or story:*

This book began with the importance of encouraging helpees to tell you stories about their life experiences. One of the most helpful things you can do is to listen carefully to stories and then summarize them back so that the client knows that he or she has been heard. This alone can sometimes lead to clients rethinking or reframing their stories from new perspectives.

But, listening may not be enough for your helpee. To change the meaning of the story may require more action on your part. You could reframe or rename the story yourself from your own perspective. Here you use a form of self-disclosure and feedback to enable a new interpretation of events. You could also reframe or rename the story using basic theory as suggested in the previous section.

But, a third way needs to be considered as well. If you engage in a conversation with your helpee on the meaning of his or her story and ask questions, the client may generate new ways of thinking about the story which lead to new solutions.

For example, let us assume that the helpee has told you a story about how very hard life has been. You listen carefully to a long list of woes and problems. These problems do indeed help explain why the helpee is sad and blue, perhaps even clinically depressed. You will likely find that if you repeat this type of negative story back to the client via a summarization that they will nod sadly in agreement. And then they will continue to think and act negatively. Something more than listening is needed!

The active skill of reframing or interpretation of negative stories occurs in a variety of ways. Listed below are a few for you to consider:

*Positive reframe*. Here you find something positive in the story to focus on.

"As I have heard your story, I note a persistence and willingness to continue despite all odds. Let's talk a bit about your persistence which I would call a 'hang in there' style. What would you name someone who continues and persists?"

This opens a dialog or conversation between you and the helpee around a new name for reflecting on the meaning of the story. Other ways to develop positive reframes include:

"What are the exceptions to the problems? When does this problem not occur? In what part of your story/problem do you take some pride and satisfaction? Can you identify someone positive in the story who supported and helped you? What did you do right? Can you build on that?"

And keep in mind that you, yourself, may need to provide the positive reframe or interpretation at times.

*Using focusing to generate multiperspective thought.* In this case the several areas of focus analysis can be used to enable the helpee to see the problem from someone else's frame of reference. As various frames are considered, the helpee may find one of them more helpful than his or her own perceptions.

The example questions are designed to be general and, of course, must be adapted and made natural as part of the interview.

*Helpee focus.* Make sure the helpee uses self-referent "I-statements."

"So, far you've talked about the problem as if it occurred somewhere else. Now, tell me the story again, but this time, use "I-statements" focusing on how you personally see and relate to the story."

*Helper focus.* Use your own frame of reference to interpret or reframe the problem or story. This can be done directly or indirectly. Note that this becomes a form of self-disclosure to aid the helpee in reframing.

"As I listen to your story, it reminds me of one of mine. I'll tell it to you briefly and then perhaps we can talk and see how it applies and doesn't apply to your story."

*Other individual's focus.* This is an important exercise in perspective taking. The helpee is encouraged to tell the story as someone else might see it.

"How would your mother (spouse, partner, friend) tell the story? What sense would they make out of it? Then we can come back to your view and see how they are similar and different."

*Problem or topic focus.* Whereas the helpee focus seeks to help the client see how he or she internalizes the problem, focus on the problem itself can sometimes help the client externalize and look at issues more clearly.

"Let's focus exclusively on the problem itself. What would you name the problem? Let's give it a specific name and talk about it from that frame."

"What is the problem doing to you? What is it doing to others? Is the problem benefitting you or someone else in some way? What can you do to conquer the problem?"

*Family focus.* This is specific way to <u>externalize</u> the problem. At times, issues will be clarified if you move away from an "I focus" and *internalization*. It often helps clients to see how their issues were and are generated in a family context.

"We learn much of our lifestyle and ways of being as individuals in a family. Tell me about your family and how they might view or handle this concern of yours. How does your way of coping relate to behaviors and styles you learned in your family of origin?"

*Cultural/environmental/context focus.* Still another way to externalize the issue is to focus on how gender/ethnic/religious/cultural styles relate to helpee concerns. All too often helpees take on more self-blame and responsibility for the problem than is merited.

"Let's think about your concern in a different way for a moment. Given your spiritual/ethnic/gender/cultural background, does this somehow relate to your issues? How does being (e.g., Baptist/Jewish, Polish/Caribbean, male/female, or Latina/European American) relate to this issue? Let's examine your concern from a cultural and contextual frame of reference."

## INTERPRETATION/REFRAMING (MICROSKILLS STRATEGY #8)

The general purpose of an interpretation is the reframing of the client's story or issue from a new perspective. You and your helpee's goal is to think—and act—differently.

Two general styles of reframing or interpretation are summarized here—helpee-directed and helper-facilitated. The first, in which the helpee finds a new way of thinking which is uniquely his or her own, is often the most powerful and lasting.

*Helpee-directed reframing.*

Your task is to enable the helpee to think in new and creative ways about the situation or issue, but the reframe comes from the helpee, not from you.

Step 1. Use the basic listening sequence to hear the client's story or issue. Summarize and repeat back what you have heard.

Step 2. Enter into a conversation with the helpee suggesting that it may be helpful to look at the situation from a fresh perspective. For example, "I've heard your story/issue. Let's talk for awhile about how you might view the matter in a fresh and new way."

Step 3. Provide questions and prompts using one or more of the following methods:

*Naming.* Draw from your listening skills and then ask, "How would you *name* or talk about the issue differently?" The idea of concrete naming of an issue with a single term or short phrase is sometimes key to looking at things in a fresh way.

*Positive reframe.* By asking questions about helpee strengths, enable the discovery of exceptions to the problem or specific things that the helpee is doing well.

"What are some things in this situation which are more positive or show some strengths on your part?"

*Focusing reframe.* This is a bit more directive in that you provide a clearer structure by asking the client to look at the problem, concern, or issue from the perspective of self, the helper, other individuals, problem or topic, family, or cultural/environmental context. "Tell me how a friend or family member would talk about the same situation." "How do you imagine I would describe what you are talking about?" "How would this situation look different if viewed from a cultural or spiritual perspective?"

The importance of a conversation with the client is important. You as helper are working with the helpee to enable the finding of a new direction.

*Helper-facilitated reframing.*

The goals are the same as above, but this time you more actively share your perceptions and ideas about the situation. Following are some specific actions you can take to facilitate reframing. Note that the first two steps are the same.

Step 1. Use the basic listening sequence to hear the client's story or issue. Summarize and repeat back what you have heard.

Step 2. Enter into a conversation with the helpee suggesting that it may be helpful to look at the situation from a fresh perspective. For example, "I've heard your story/ issue. Let's talk for awhile about how you might view the matter in a fresh and new way." Please note that some theoretical orientations would prefer that you work with a bit more distance from the helpee and not talk about the idea of a co-generated conversation. Regardless, in helper facilitated reframing, you are taking more responsibility for the new name and frame of reference.

Step 3. Use one of the following methods to share your new perspective of the situation, problem, or issue.

*Naming.* Providing a new name via a short phrase or single word can be one of the most powerful reframes. For example, renaming depression as a logical response to societal sexism frees many women to look at their lives differently.

*Positive reframing.* Many times, helpees will have difficulty in finding strengths. You will have to point out their capabilities many times. Sometimes a major issue is working with the helpee so that he or she can accept your more positive view.

*Focusing reframing.* Here you are called on to use the concept of focus and tell the story which the helpee may not have been able to tell. This may be especially so when it comes to cultural/environmental/contextual issues. The naming of depression as sexism, the naming of a dysfunction as a result of an alcoholic family, the naming of hypertension as a logical result of racism or demands from the family for success are some examples of different ways to focus on helpee concerns.

*Theoretical reframing.* As you advance in the helping profession, you will want to help clients reframe their ideas from many different theoretical orientations.

Intergenerational family theory. "Your issue seems to relate to your family history" followed by the specific examples in history and the present.

Cognitive-behavioral. "Your negative thoughts about yourself are irrational ideas. Let me explain. . . . "

Psychoanalytic. "Your dream seems to go back to childhood experience."

Humanistic. "I hear you talking negatively about yourself. But from another perspective, I hear a person who tries very hard to measure up and be good, but at a large personal price."

# INTERPRETATION/REFRAMING

---

**The check-out is critical**. With any reframe or interpretation, checking out with the client how the new idea was received is critical. This keeps the conversation open. For example, ask the helpee, "How do you react to that?" "How does that sound?" "Is that interpretation close?" "Do you like that frame of reference?" If he or she agrees, you have at least some indication you are on track. If they disagree, you have immediate and useful data indicating you need to try some other approach to reframing.

Interpretation has too long been viewed as a mystical activity in which the interviewer reaches into the depths of the helpee's personality and provides a brilliant new insight. However, if you see interpretation as the reframing of old ideas into a new pattern or way of thinking and behaving, the skill loses much of its mystery. Yet, perhaps even a new power is gained.

The power to name and rename the world around us is profound. Use this power wisely in conversation with your helpees.

## VIEWING OF A VIDEOTAPE OR LIVE DEMONSTRATION OF INTERPRETATION/REFRAMING

The Feedback Sheet on the following page can be used to make notes on the video or live demonstration on interpretation/reframing. This same form may also be used for your own practice sessions.

## FEEDBACK SHEET FOR INTERPRETATION/REFRAMING

1. How does the interview draw out the basic situation or story using the basic listening sequence?

2. How does the helper first try to engage the helpee in a conversation and enable the discovery of new ways of thinking about the situation?

3. Was helpee-reframing attempted and how effective was it? Naming? Positive reframe? Focusing reframe? Was the check-out used?

---

4. Did the helper directly involve himself or herself in reframing? Naming? Positive reframe? Focusing reframe? Theoretically-oriented reframe? Was the check-out used?

5. Active mastery. Did the client actually generate a new and workable frame of reference either by herself or himself or with the aid of the helper? Does that new frame of reference seem useful to you? Do you think the helpee may actually act on it?

## PRACTICING THE SKILL OF INTERPRETATION

1. Develop a working group for practice.

2. Assign roles for the session and plan for the interview.

Client.       It would be useful if you were willing to share an issue of interpersonal conflict. However, any of the patterns listed in Manual #8 may be used.

Interviewer.  Your task is as follows:

a. Draw out the concern using the basic listening sequence.

b. Search for a repeating pattern. Help the client identify the behavior/thought/etc. as pattern. (This is a form of interpretation.)

c. Provide one or more alternative interpretations of the situation/behavior/pattern from your own frame of reference.

Observer.     Again, keep a verbatim log of the interviewer's statements. Provide feedback using the form provided for the videotape demonstration session. To ensure clarity, you will find that following the specific five steps of the videotape viewing guide on the preceding page will prove to be a useful format for feedback.

3. Provide feedback and rotate roles.

## GENERALIZATION PLAN

This is a skill which does not come easily. It is complex, and operates differently in different theories. Take some time and give thought to what specific aspects of the chapter you might want to follow up on first. Will you follow a plan to make your interpretations/reframes more impactful on clients?

We also suggest that you find a friend who may have a concern (not serious) which he or she would like to explore with you. Before you start, tell them a bit about the potential value of reframing. Make it a real conversation as the two of you work together to find new says to look at the situation. Sometimes it is helpful to have the list of possible styles of interpretations/reframes available with you and to share it with your friend.

# CHAPTER 8

# INTEGRATION OF SKILLS:

### GENERATING AN INFINITE NUMBER OF RESPONSES
### THE FIVE-STAGE INTERVIEW
### ASSERTIVENESS TRAINING

How are you going to recall, master, and integrate the many skills and strategies which have been presented in this book? Through a step-by-step method, you have encountered the basic language and skills of interviewing, counseling, and therapy. It is now your task to integrate skills in your own natural fashion.

This chapter offers you several tasks, all of which can help you develop an integrated mastery of the interview. We suggest that it is vital that you first start from a base which you believe in and with which you are personally comfortable. Then, we ask you to take another look: How can you add additional skills and strategies which "stretch" you a bit, but may be useful at some point in the future when you find your own natural style not quite "reaching" the client or helpee?

This chapter seeks to encourage you to:

1. Generate an infinite number of helping responses which you will have available for any client statement, even the most challenging.

2. Examine the five-stage interviewing model as a basic for structuring effective helping sessions.

3. Engage in a basic assertiveness training interview.

4. Generate a transcript of one (or more) of your interviews as you start the process of developing an increasingly sophisticated natural helping style which is distinctly your own.

## GENERATING AN INFINITE NUMBER OF HELPING RESPONSES

One of the best ways to review and summarize the many skills and strategies of this book is to take a sample client statement and write helping responses which might be used with that client. Following are two possible interviewing scenarios which your helpee might present.

Alternatively, you may want to write a statement describing some of your own personal issues and see how many responses you can generate to your concerns. Perhaps you may think of a helpee you currently have or may have in the future—how would he or she talk about personal concerns? Or, you may have a "nightmare" of what a client may say to you in the interview.

Select one of the two below or write a short possible client script to which you could respond.

1. I'm really worried about how I'm doing in school. I started the term in pretty good shape, but then my kids got sick. I couldn't afford a sitter, so I missed some classes and now I'm terribly behind. Then last week, the car broke down on the way here. How can I put things together at this point? I think the teachers are being unfair to me by not considering what's going on in my life—they really tick me off. They act as if my school issues are my fault!

2. I can't stand it anymore (near tears). The kids are really giving me a bad time about me being gay and all that stuff. Joe and Sam are pushing me around in the hall. One of my best friends won't come over any more. My mom seems to accept me, but Dad won't have anything to do with me. The P.E. teacher called me a "freak" in front of the class. I want to be "gay and proud." I knew it was going to be tough when I decided to come out, but not this bad.

3. Your own script:

_____

_____

_____

_____

_____

_____

1. Within microtraining skills the first response to consider is the potential for attending or non-attending (topic-jump) responses.

   *An attending response is* _____

   *A non-attending response is* _____

2. Using the several attending skills, develop alternative attending responses with focus on the helpee.

   *Closed question* _____

   *Open question* _____

   *Minimal encourager* _____

   *Paraphrase* _____

_Reflection of feeling_ _____

_____

_Summarization_ (for this response you need to imagine other data previously presented by the helpee) _____

_____

_____

3. Write two confrontation statements.

a. _____

b. _____

4. Write three possible different directives you could use.

a. _____

b. _____

c. _____

5. Provide some feedback for the client.

_____

_____

_____

6. What might you self-disclose which would be potentially useful?

_____

_____

_____

7. What are two alternative interpretations from two differing frames of reference?

a. _____

b. _____

8. Not only can any microtraining skill be potentially appropriate, but the focus of the helpee statement could be on any of the six categories presented. Present six interpretations, paraphrases, or other microtraining skills with varying foci.

*Client* _____

*Helper* (on you) _____

_____

*Other individuals* _____

_____

*Problem, concern, or topic* _____

_____

*Family* _____

_____

*Cultural-environmental-context* _____

_____

_____

9. What would be some advice/information/instruction/explanation which you might give to the client? Used carefully and sparingly, advice can be helpful.

_____

_____

_____

Given the several microtraining skills, the six dimensions of focus, and the many differing theoretical orientations, it should be obvious that there is an infinite array of possibilities to respond to any client. The effectiveness of the counseling leads you use is not measured by the quality of your statement, but rather by what the client does in response to what you say or do.

Your task is to learn many responses, note your client, and then move with the client's special needs. As there are so many different possibilities for responding to a client, it is helpful to have theory to organize your approaches to helping and it may be observed that vastly different sets of microskills may be used with various theories. You will find that if you have mastered the basic microskills and the structure of the interview following, you have an excellent tool for rapidly learning the many alternatives to interviewing practice.

## THE FIVE-STAGE INTERVIEW (MICROSKILLS STRATEGY #9)

What makes for an effective interview? It could be said that all our clients in some way come to us to discuss their issues and concerns and solve their problems. A well-formed session may be related to the classical decision-making or problem-solving framework:

1. Define the problem.
2. Generate alternatives for solution.
3. Decide on one alternative for action.

This three-part model is expanded in microskill training to the following five dimensions. For example, in the interview, we really need to start problem solving first with a solid relationship between helper and helpee. The five-stage model also stresses the importance of goal setting as a separate issue.

Often you will go over the following five stages in order, but at other times it is important to be flexible, move around, and consider the five aspects a "checklist" so that you are sure to cover all the necessary aspects.

The five-stage interview will help you organize the interview. Too often helpers and clients wander about in an aimless, directionless interview. Stage 3—goal setting—may be the most important new concept of the five stages. If you and your client agree on goals for an interview, both of you can refer back to them from time to time to be sure you are progressing in a meaningful direction. (And, if necessary, the goals can easily be changed.)

The following chart summarizes the five stages. It stresses the importance of rapport building and structuring the interview at the beginning. With most clients you will first listen to the problem or concern, but also give considerable attention to positive strengths.

Goal setting, Stage 3, has just been described as central to an interview with direction. With some clients, you may want to do goal setting at the beginning of

# INTEGRATION OF SKILLS

| Definition of stage | Function and purpose of stage | Commonly used skills |
|---|---|---|
| 1. Rapport and structuring. "Hello." | To build a working alliance with the client and to enable the client to feel comfortable with the interviewer. Structuring may be needed to explain the purpose of the interview. Structuring functions to help keep the session on task and to inform the client what the counselor can and cannot do. | Attending behavior to establish contact with the client, and client observation skills to determine appropriate methods to build rapport. Structuring most often involves the influencing skill of information giving and instructions. |
| 2. Gathering information, defining the problem, and identifying assets. "What's your concern?" | To find out why the client has come to the interview and how he or she views the problem. Skillful problem definition will help avoid aimless topic jumping and give the interview purpose and direction. Also to identify clearly positive strengths of the client. | Most common are the attending skills, especially the basic listening sequence. Other skills may be used as necessary. If problems aren't clear, you may need more influencing skills. The positive asset search often reveals capabilities in the client that are useful in finding problem resolution. |
| 3. Determining outcomes. Where does the client want to go? "What do you want to have happen?" | To find out the ideal world of the client. How would the client like to be? How would things be if the problem were solved? This stage is important in that it enables the interviewer to know what the client wants. The desired direction of the client and counselor should be reasonably harmonious. With some clients, skip phase 2 and define goals first. | Most common are the attending skills, especially the basic listening sequence. Other skills used as necessary. If outcome is still unclear, more influencing skills may be helpful. With clients from other cultures and those who are less verbal, this phase should often precede phase 2. Solution oriented counseling stresses the importance of this stage. |
| 4. Exploring alternatives and confronting client incongruities. "What are we going to do about it?" | To work toward resolution of the client's issue. This may involve the creative problem-solving model of generating alternatives and deciding among those alternatives. It also may involve lengthy exploration of personal dynamics. This phase of the interview may be the longest. | May begin with a summary of the major discrepancies. Depending on the issue and theory of the interviewer, a heavy use of influencing skills may be expected. Attending skills still used for balance. |
| 5. Generalization and transfer of learning. "Will you do it?" | To enable changes in thoughts, feelings, and behaviors in the client's daily life. Many clients go through an interview and then do nothing to change their behavior, remaining in the same world they came from. | Influencing skills, such as directives and information/explanation, are particularly important. Attending skills used to check out client understanding of importance of the stage. |

From *Intentional Interviewing and Counseling*, by Allen E. Ivey. Copyright © 1994 by Wadsworth, Inc. Reprinted by permission of Brooks/Cole Publishing Company. Monterey, California.

the interview. Finally, give sufficient attention to finding solutions and ensuring that clients and helpees work on taking ideas from the interview back home.

Interestingly, you will find it possible to use the same five stages of the interview to *plan* an interview before it happens. Specifically, it is useful to think ahead about alternative ways you might work on better rapport with a client. After one or more interviews, it is useful to use the five-stage framework to plan longer-term treatment goals. The problems of the client and the several goals may be listed using the same framework and the several treatment alternatives listed in stage 4. Finally, specific plans for generalization of learned behavior should be included in any treatment or interviewing series.

Summary notes for practicum and for agency records may be kept in a similar five-stage format. There is a marked advantage of simplicity and directness in this framework which can be used in many theoretical orientations.

## ASSERTIVENESS TRAINING (MICROSKILLS STRATEGY #10)

Assertiveness training is a useful way to help clients express themselves more clearly. Assertiveness, however, is not aggressiveness. What is sought is a personal style in which the individual takes a reasonable approach to meeting needs, while considering the rights of others. Assertiveness training is an important strategy and needs to be available to interviewers and counselors when appropriate to the client situation.

The five-stage structure of the interview can be useful in understanding how to conduct assertiveness training in a personally respectful manner.

1. *Rapport and structuring.* Develop rapport with your client in your usual fashion. State that the purpose of this session is to explore assertiveness training in the hope that examining specific behaviors will be helpful to the client. It is important to tell the client at the outset that you will be asking them to role-play their concerns, not just talk about them.

2. *Gathering information, defining the problem, and identifying assets*. First, verbally draw out the client's story using the Basic Listening Sequence. While you must listen respectfully, storytelling is not the aim of this session—examining specific behavior and changing that behavior is the goal.

After you have heard the story, ask the client to role-play part or all of the story. You may need to play the boss or coworker, sibling, the partner, the spouse, the parent, or other "person of concern." Make the situation very specific. Then each of you speak in the role-play the main words that would be used in the real situation. For example, if the client has a conflict with a parent, find a very specific conflict situation which occurred recently. Role-play that situation in detail.

Often clients will prefer to say, "I would have said . . . " rather than talking to you directly in the present tense. Help clients achieve maximum reality. They can guide you as to the style of the other person whose role you play.

At the conclusion of the role-play, ask the client how he or she felt during the role-play. Here you can often touch on emotional experience which may be missing in verbal counseling sessions. Also ask what he or she observed. Pay attention to strengths and positive assets.

3. *Determining outcomes*. Review the role-play together in detail. Focus on observable behaviors and what was actually happening. Many interviews can get bogged down in analyzing rather than paying attention to what is happening concretely.

Goal setting in assertiveness training focuses on change in behavior. For example, in dealing with a difficult boss who gives confusing directions, avoid talking about why the helpee backs down so quickly. Rather focus on lack of eye contact, apologizing words, and backing up. The goals in this example could be direct eye contact, staying in place, and assertively asking the boss specifically what he or she wants done.

Do not continue to the next stage until very clear, observable, behavioral goals have been specified. You will also find that the positive asset search can be used to strengthen client self-confidence.

4. *Exploring alternatives and confronting incongruity.*

Now that specific behavioral goals have been selected, engage in another role-play. Most clients will only succeed partially in this first try. It is important to discuss the partial success and reward beginning levels of change. But, it is most important that you continue with more role-plays until the person fully masters the new behavioral skills.

You will find that the basics of effective assertiveness often lie in appropriate eye contact, body language, vocal tone, and directness and clarity in verbal expression—the foundation skills of attending behavior.

When the client has been successful, congratulate her or him and support the behavior change. You may want to do a verbal review and analysis of change at that time.

5. *Generalization.* It is most important that you talk about specifics of behavioral transfer to the real situation. At times, this may require additional role-plays to cement the learning. Make arrangements with your client for follow-up either in person or by phone so that they can continue to feel your encouragement and support.

## OBSERVATION OF VIDEO DEMONSTRATION OF THE FIVE STAGES AND INTEGRATION OF SKILLS

The first video example demonstrates a brief vocational interview. The five stages are identified one by one. Remember that this demonstration is compressed for illustrative purposes for obviously more time would be required for a full session.

The second video demonstration focuses on assertiveness training using the same five-stage model. An assertiveness training session will not always go that smoothly or quickly.

Study the two interviews for integration of skills and structure while maintaining awareness that they are demonstrations. In your own practice sessions, you will want to have more time to explore the several stages one by one, but experience reveals that following the five-stage structure in the early stages will be most helpful in developing a successful interviewing style in the long run.

# INTEGRATION OF SKILLS

---

## INTERVIEW INTEGRATION FEEDBACK FORM

1. Rapport:




2. Defining the problem and identifying assets:




3. Determining outcomes:




4. Exploration of alternatives and confronting incongruity:




5. Generalization and transfer of learning from the interview:

## PRACTICING INTEGRATION OF SKILLS

There are three basic competencies in skill integration.

1. The ability to conduct an interview using only attending skills and the basic listening sequence. This is the basic competency sought in *Basic Attending Skills training*. (If you have not yet completed this exercise, you may wish to do so before conducting a full interview using influencing skills.)

2. The ability to conduct an interview balancing the several attending and influencing skills over the five stages.

3. The ability to produce specific client action as a result of your interview. Give special attention to the generalization stage and follow up to determine the effectiveness of your session. Does the client act on any alternatives generated?

For the practice session:

1. Divide into pairs, or, if time permits, move to groups of four so that an observer is available.

2. Assign roles for the practice session:

Client:    Select an area where you are either too aggressive or insufficiently assertive. This may be in failing to speak up in a class, letting someone in front of you in line, or being too aggressive in your sales technique. Before you start, let the helper know your general topic. Alternatively, discuss a vocational planning issue.

Helper:    Conduct an interview following the five-stage model. You may wish to conduct an assertiveness training session such as that on the video modeling tape . . . or you may wish to conduct a problem-solving interview on your own. Give special attention to the final phase—generalization and transfer of learning. Develop a working contract with your client so that he or she actually plans to do something. Then, plan to follow up on the client the next week to find out what happened.

Observer:   Use the five-stage form to provide feedback for the interview.

3. Conduct a full interview, provide sufficient feedback and analysis, and rotate roles.

## BASIC FORM FOR INTERVIEWING PLAN, FEEDBACK ON AN ACTUAL INTERVIEW, WRITING A REPORT ON THE INTERVIEW, AND DEVELOPING A LONG-TERM TREATMENT PLAN

| | |
|---|---|
| *1. Rapport/ structuring* | Special issues around rapport development. What need to structure this interview do you have? Do you plan a specific theory? Skill sequence? |
| *2. Problem definition and identification of assets* | What are the anticipated problems for this client? Strengths? How do you plan to define the problem with the client? |
| *3. Defining outcomes* | Where do you believe this client would like to go? How will you bring out the idealized self or world? |
| *4. Exploring alternatives/ confronting incongruity* | What types of alternatives should be generated? What theories would you likely use? What specific incongruities have you noted or do you anticipate in the client? What skills are you likely to use? Skill sequences? |
| *5. Generalization* | What specific plans, if any, do you have for transfer of training? What will enable you personally to feel that the interview was worthwhile? Make the contract specific and follow up the coming week to see if the client followed up on the agreement. This is the measure of active mastery. |

From *Intentional Interviewing and Counseling*, by Allen E. Ivey. Copyright © 1994 by Wadsworth, Inc. Reprinted by permission of Brooks/Cole Publishing Company, Monterey, California.

## DEVELOPING YOUR OWN INTERVIEW TYPESCRIPT AND ANALYSIS

The most effective generalization and transfer of learning which can come from this chapter is your taking the ideas and making them work for you personally. The following steps are suggested:

1. Conduct a 15-minute to half-hour interview. Find a volunteer client who will talk about a real concern or problem.

2. Develop an interview plan using the five-stage interview model.

3. Conduct the interview recording it on video or audiotape. Ask your volunteer client for permission to record the interview. Point out that he or she may have the recorder turned off at any time. Most people do not object to being recorded and this is especially so if you remain relaxed about it yourself. If your first session does not go through the five stages, find another client and try again.

4. Make a typescript of the tape. Insofar as possible, divide the typescript into the five basic segments of the interviewing plan. Classify your leads and note which types of microskills you use most frequently and their impact on the client. At the end of each interviewing stage, comment on your effectiveness and what happened.

5. Develop a summary of the interview using the same basic five stages. This could serve as a report to a practicum adviser, or the file in a community agency. As part of generalization phase, follow up with your client a week later and report whether or not he or she did anything which developed from the interview. Did your work generalize? The best test of an interviewer is what the client does and thinks after the session is over.

6. Provide your own subjective comments on the session, analysis of your total skill usage. Did you use more attending than influencing skills? Did you avoid interpretation or use it extensively?

# CHAPTER 9

# TEACHING HELPING SKILLS TO OTHERS*

This chapter is for the instructor and for those students who want to teach communication skills to others. Microcounseling is a scaled-down interviewing session in which a beginning counselor talks with a volunteer client about real problems. The interview occurs in a setting which provides interviewing practice with maximum opportunity for immediate feedback and trainee growth. The compressed nature of the situation allows a focus on specific dimensions of interviewing skills and does not demand that the trainee respond immediately as a fully professional counselor.

Microcounseling methods are derived from basic social learning principles. Participants receive cognitive cueing about the skills they are to learn, see the skill in action, read about it, and then practice the skill. This method is effective not only in teaching skills of helping and interviewing, but also in teaching clients communication skills. Skill training is an alternative counseling form in itself.

Thus the objectives of the video and written materials are double: to teach specific skills and to provide methods by which those who have learned the skills can transmit them to others.

## MASTERY GOALS

As a teacher, trainer, or one who teaches communication skills to clients, you may want to keep the basic mastery goals of this book in mind. The most important issue is, "Does the client do something different as a result of your action?" The

---

*This chapter repeats introductory information from *Basic Attending Skills*, as the instructional method is similar. New, however, are concepts of active mastery of skills. Certain parts of this section are taken from the book *Microcounseling: Innovations in Interviewing Training* by Allen E. Ivey. Permission to quote and paraphrase certain portions of the book was granted by the publisher, Charles C. Thomas, 301 East Lawrence Avenue, Springfield, Illinois 62717.

specific mastery goals are summarized in Chapter 1 and at the beginning of each chapter. Issues are raised around active mastery in each of the small group practice sessions. Experience has revealed that trainees learn the skills more rapidly and effectively if the mastery goals are kept before them. The *intentional* use of microskills is manifested when one thinks ahead about what one wants to have happen and it happens.

The concept of active mastery is new to microcounseling. In the past, basic mastery or simple demonstration of the ability to use the skill in the interview was all that was called for. Active mastery demands the ability to make something happen.

Nowhere is active mastery more important than in the five stages of the interview. The concept of active mastery coupled with the generalization and transfer of learning phase of the five phases of the interview helps beginning (and experienced) helpers think more effectively about what they are doing in the interview and its immediate impact.

Now, let us turn to some general implications of workshops for training others in microskills.

## INTRODUCTORY COMMENTS ON WORKSHOPS

*What populations are the workshops for?* We have tried to write materials and design videotape mini-lectures and models so the workshop may be suitable for a variety of people. The structure of this book is designed for college students. Beginning helpers, teachers, parents, peer counselors, psychiatric aides, nurses, minority advocates, and high school students represent only a sampling of the wide variety of populations with whom these workshops have proven successful.

Although these workshops can be used with a wide variety of trainee populations, it must be recognized that the examples and video models tend to represent middle-class concepts and values. These materials, however, have been used successfully with a variety of trainees. Despite this fact, the leader/trainer may wish to adapt these materials and supplement them with specific examples more relevant to minority or special group concerns.

With a more advanced group—for example, clinical psychology trainees, medical students, and counselor educators—these same materials can and have been used. The vocabulary of the leader changes and adaptations of some exercises may be necessary. However, when working with such groups, the stress is on the *teaching role* of the professional. Advanced students appear to enjoy and benefit most from a workshop such as this when they consider whether or not such a method may be useful to them in teaching helping skills to others. The professional helper is increasingly called upon to run workshops and present ideas about human interaction to many groups. The concepts of active mastery will be new to most experienced people and provide an interesting challenge.

*For how many is this workshop designed?* These workshops were planned for use with groups of approximately 20 people. However, they could be used with as few as one or two or with groups of up to 200 or more with appropriate adaptations.

A workshop could be managed with one leader and one videotape machine. The specificity of exercises and peer feedback gives virtually every participant a chance for significant experiential and cognitive participation. Ideally, however, one leader for each 10–12 people is better. It is possible for the senior leader to train assistant leaders from the trainee population before the formal workshop.

Whether these tapes and materials are used in one-to-one counselor training or in workshop format, it is highly desirable that all participants have allotted time wherein they can practice videotaping counseling sessions outside of the immediate training situation. We have found that peer supervision is effective in supplementing formal microcounseling training.

*What is the training outline?*

Each workshop may be structured with the following steps.

1. *Warm-up/orientation*  The introductory pages of the chapter may be read. An elementary exercise may be used to warm up individuals for the workshop or training they are about to receive.

2. *Reading*  Each chapter contains a microcounseling manual defining the skill. We suggest that the participants read these brief manuals before viewing the videotape (or reading the typescript if the video is unavailable).

3. *Viewing of video model or a live demonstration by the instructor*  Each skill is demonstrated so that participants can see the skill in action. If the videotape is not available, it is suggested that you as trainer do a "live" demonstration.

4. *Practice*  Specific suggestions for practicing the skill are included in each chapter. It should be possible to go over these practice instructions with the trainees carefully in the early sessions of training. Then, when they have more experience, the groups will basically "run themselves." Note skill feedback sheets for each chapter.

5. *Generalization*  Some workshop leaders fail to use this portion of microcounseling which helps ensure behavioral learning and retention. Note the recommendations for generalization in Chapter 2 and with each succeeding skill develop specific steps for your group to take the concept beyond the session. It is helpful to assign homework. Audiotapes or typescripts of each skill may be required so that the participant specifically demonstrates basic mastery or active mastery.

Chapter 8, Integration of Skills, follows a somewhat more complex pattern and will be reviewed in more detail later.

*Is it necessary to follow the precise ordering and procedures of these workshops?* We firmly believe that each leader/trainer must adapt the suggested exercises to fit unique personality styles and situations. Those experienced in workshop development will want to change exercises and the order of activities almost immediately. Those just starting this type of workshop may want to follow the guidelines fairly precisely the first few times, but will later move to personal adaptations.

Our experience is that the general type of format presented here is usually quite successful with groups. It provides a reasonable balance of cognitive input with practice and time for people to be together with people. A variety of activities are suggested, thus keeping the group moving on to different things, thus maintaining interest and involvement.

Sometimes when running a workshop, you will find when you are either beginning or halfway through that the group has another agenda more pressing to them than learning the specific skills you want to teach. It is here that leader/trainer flexibility is most important. Structurally, there are three options open to the leader when the group seems to have a need different from your objectives. As one possibility, the leader can "go with the group" and change the role to that of encounter/facilitator to group process with the result that the skill emphasis of the workshop will be lost. At another extreme, the leader can stay on schedule and state that those other issues should be examined in another time and place.

We would suggest a middle course between these two extremes. If the group has difficulty working through their personal relationships, the leader can suggest that these issues then become the data for the skills sessions. It should be noted, however, that when a helper is personally involved in the issue, it is difficult to listen carefully as demanded in these listening skill sessions. If the participants can try out newly learned skills on issues meaningful to them, maximum learning and behavioral transfer can occur.

At a minimum, each leader must be prepared to adapt materials as the workshop progresses. No one way is right. With experience, the "sense of the group" can be developed and exercises arranged to fit these needs as they appear.

*How much time does it take to cover the basic workshop?* With a tight schedule, it is possible to complete the nine basic workshops in nine two-hour sessions. This is a good framework when you have able, hard-working people who want to learn a maximum of information in a minimum of time. The problem with this intensive approach is that time for practice sessions is minimized and serious negotiation on the "do-use-teach" contracts becomes almost impossible.

Thus 30 hours to part of a term seems a more appropriate time to cover the information provided here. The extra time should be given primarily to providing individuals with a substantial amount of practice in the skills.

Originally we had suggested specific lengths of time for each exercise. We found through experience that some exercises can take ten minutes with one group and two hours with another. As such, the leader will have to select exercises and adapt them to fit the special needs and interests of each group.

*Ethical questions.* The workshop trainer should remember that we are working with people and usual standards for ethical conduct for training in counseling and group procedures hold. The *Microcounseling* text provides a discussion of ethical issues in microcounseling. Perhaps most important is the trainer being available to provide support and follow-up for any individual who needs or desires further counseling assistance.

At this point it seems appropriate to turn to specific suggestions for teaching each chapter of the book. We have found that the model provided is effective and useful in many settings including professional, paraprofessional, and peer volunteer programs.

## TEACHING SUGGESTIONS FOR CHAPTER 1

As this is the first training session, it is suggested that time be spent in first acquainting people with the general microskills training model:

1. *Getting acquainted.* Divide your group in pairs and have participants introduce one another. Provide time in pairs to get acquainted. You may want to use a favorite name game or activity.

2. *Group expectations.* Move to groups of four. Use this time for the members of your group to become better acquainted. Then, pass out newsprint (or appoint a recorder for each group) and ask participants to state the expectations/ needs/wants for the training session, workshop, or course.

3. *What would you say?* The first chapter exercise may be completed and participants should write down what they want to say to the client described there. Ask the groups of four to share what they have written down. You may want to show a videotape of a client or present a role-play with the same objective. The critical point is that people note that virtually everyone would respond differently to the client.

4. *Workshop outline.* Present the microskills hierarchy and the several skills of the workshop. You may want to assess differential experience levels in your group and which individuals should seek basic mastery and which active mastery. Give special attention to the mastery level concepts.

5. *Ethics and confidentiality.* In small groups, individuals may share their personal expectations for sharing and expectations for confidentiality, etc. Develop a group consensus for ethics. One of the most important rules is that no one should share anything they do not wish and that anyone may stop sharing or self-disclosing at any time. Keep yourself available throughout the workshop for discussion and referral.

6. *Mini-lecture on millipede effect.* Read over and present the concepts of the millipede effect. Ask your group how they might have experienced awkwardness with single skills. Emphasize eventual skill integration and the active mastery concept once again.

7. *Cross-cultural differences.* Point out how attending behavior plays itself out differently among different cultures. For example, eye contact patterns differ from group to group. Elicit information on cross-cultural differences from your group. You may find it helpful to have each member identify him or herself ethnically and share similarities and differences among cultural groups.

8. *Summarize the goals and methods of the training program in your own words.*

9. *Typescript assignment.* It is highly recommended that you assign each member to audiorecord a brief interviewing session with their natural interviewing style before the remainder of the session begins.

## SUGGESTIONS FOR CHAPTERS 2–8

The following model has been tested in many different situations through clinical testing and empirical research. It works! But, you must change the concepts to meet the needs of yourself and your group. We will go through the model in detail and you can refer to this outline as you move through the several chapters.

1. *Warm-up/orientation.* Go through the objectives of the chapter. Discuss the active mastery concepts as a goal to strive for. Each chapter begins with an elementary exercise to personalize the skill. For example, Chapter 2 asks participants to identify characteristics of helping people. Divide your group into triads or fours to discuss the answers to the warm-up piece.

2. *Reading.* Read the microcounseling strategy(ies). It may seem absurd to read quietly alone in a workshop. However, some people learn most effectively in

this mode. It gives participants a chance to deal with the skill area in their own way. It also provides cognitive cueing so that videotape viewing is better understood.

3. *Videotape viewing.* If you do not have a videotape, conduct a role-played or audiotaped session as a demonstration of the skill. Have participants note what they observe in the space provided in the manual. Discuss these observations in the large group, but not in excessive detail. Practice is what the workshop is about.

4. *Practice the skill.* Divide into groups of two, three, or four. Fours appear to be most fruitful, but smaller groups provide more practice. Follow these steps carefully, especially until your group becomes used to them.

    a. Read the practice instructions with them. Do each step one at a time. Be sure that people are in groups before you assign roles. Check topics for clients carefully—they are important. Review constantly. The model works, but is confusing to first-time participants.

    b. Allow 3–7 minutes for practicing the skill.

    c. Allow about twice as much time for debriefing and feedback as practice time.

    d. Hold time firmly and rotate roles regularly.

    e. Check with participants in groups on identification, basic, and active mastery.

5. *Generalization.* Study the generalization material of Chapter 2 carefully. Each session works best if you follow-up with homework, typescripts, and various exercises to prevent relapse and failure to learn and use skills. Requiring each person to teach the skill to someone each week is a useful generalization technique.

Individual variation with each chapter should be added. Here are some key issues in each chapter for you to consider:

*Chapter 2. Basic listening sequence.* Be sure that both the story and the positive asset search are fully brought out. Can the individuals bring out the facts, feelings, and organization of the problem? They will do this again and again as they move later to the influencing skills. Active mastery is critical here.

*Chapter 3. Focus.* Trainees should not rush, but take sufficient time to draw out multiple stories and multiple perspectives.

*Chapter 4. Confrontation.* Have participants show that they understand the concepts of incongruity, discrepancy, and conflict before they actually start trying the confrontation skill. Confrontation is basically a complex skill using the basic listening skills and focusing. Emphasize the stock phrase, "On one hand . . . , but on the other . . . " It may seem trite, but it is a good way to sharpen and clarify the skill. Individuals later will become unique and drop the stock phrase.

*Chapter 5. Directives.* It is important in this workshop to provide individual practice in each of the directives before moving to small group practice. We find it helpful to divide participants into pairs and talk about a time when they were procrastinating. Then, one member of the pair gives some advice and you, as leader, obtain reactions to that advice. Sometimes the reactions are positive, sometimes they are negative. Then you can demonstrate the several types of possible directives and your participants can practice each one after you have demonstrated. For example, you demonstrate with a client the paradoxical directive "Continue procrastinating . . . " and then participants can try it. Then demonstrate guided imagery and participants can try it. *Select those directives which are appropriate to your group level of experience.*

In the practice session (and in the rest of the sessions on influencing skills), stress the importance of using the basic listening sequence *before* attempting the influencing skill. At least briefly define the facts, feelings, and organization of the client's problem before providing a directive, self-disclosure, etc.

*Chapter 6. Feedback and self-disclosure.* Note carefully that two skills are taught and practiced in the session. Have participants follow the practice instructions carefully.

*Chapter 7. Interpretation/reframing.* This may be divided into two workshops. The creativity exercise can be extended and you may wish to teach the first session on the concept of frame of reference by itself.

The practice instructions for this session provide two different objectives: a) to develop interpretations and new names for old situations, and b) to practice reframing a situation using positive and negative examples within a pattern.

Additional teaching suggestions and ideas may be found in the several books referenced in Chapter 1, particularly Ivey's *Intentional/Interviewing and Counseling.*

## SUGGESTIONS FOR CHAPTER 8

1. *How many responses can you develop for a single helpee statement?* Divide your group into triads or fours and have them work through the several responses. It is a useful summary exercise and provides an opportunity for participants to demonstrate identification mastery.

2. *Silent reading of Microcounseling Strategy #9 on the five stages of the interview.* Stress that different cultures use the stages differently. Similarly, some individuals will want to work their way through problem solving differently. This is a conceptual framework, not a definitive road map. However, beginning students who use this model find it most advantageous.

3. *View videotape model or demonstration of the structure of the interview.* There are two examples for you to choose from—vocational counseling and assertion training. When using the vocational tape, we divide the group into pairs. We show one segment of the tape—for example, rapport. The tape is stopped and the pairs do the rapport segment. This is followed by feedback and then the next segment on gathering data is shown. After each segment, the tape is stopped and the pairs practiced. This is perhaps our favorite and most effective exercise.

4. *Practice of integration of skills.* Note the basic competencies in this section. You may wish to have participants review the videotape in *Basic Attending Skills* in which a demonstration of how to use *only* attending skills in a problem-solving interview is made. Also note the importance of clients actually doing something as a result of the interview.

5. *Assign a typescript as suggested in the workshop.* This is particularly helpful in self-understanding, integration of the skills, and generalization.

## HOW TO TEACH SKILLS—CHAPTER 9

The most important use of skill training may be in teaching others (parents, patients, counselees, students) communication skills. We have found that this may be done even in a workshop setting using the following sequence:

1. Divide your group, regardless of size, into groups of four.

2. Two people in each group will select a skill that they would like to teach the other pair. The other two people select a skill they would like to teach to the first pair.

3. Planning time of about 30 minutes is allotted. During this time, the pairs plan a workshop consisting of: a) a warm-up exercise, b) reading this book coupled with some didactic presentation, c) live modeling of the skill, and d) supervised practice using feedback sheets.

4. The pair presents its skill workshop to the other pair.

5. The roles reverse.

We have found that an interesting teaching experience which reassures beginners that they actually can teach others counseling and communication skills is completed successfully in about two hours. Trainees are then prepared to go out and teach these skills beyond the workshops to parents, teachers, children, professionals, and a wide array of groups.

## THE TYPESCRIPT: A FINAL COMMENT

An all-too-common tendency in counseling training is for the trainer to present information and assume that competency in the concept will develop. This is not necessarily so.

We require students to bring in typescripts or audiotapes weekly. In these tapes they demonstrate that they can use the skill in question for positive client benefit. Such presentations take time to examine and provide feedback, yet their benefit for trainee growth cannot be denied.

At the conclusion of our course of training, we like to have our students present an interview typescript in which they demonstrate that they can conduct an interview and discuss some of the theoretical implications of their demonstrated helping practices. The value of a typescript analysis cannot be over emphasized.

---

## FEEDBACK FORM ON INFLUENCING

Name _____ Skill area evaluated _____
                    (Optional)

1. One thing (if any) in my behavior which I plan to change as a result of this session is:




2. One thing in my behavior in this series which I want to continue and see as a strength is:




3. The most helpful incident in this training was:




4. If I were conducting this training, one thing I would add would be:




5. As a result of using this skill, I was able to facilitate a real or role-played client to change in the following way, thus demonstrating active mastery:




6. Use facing page for additional comments and/or suggestions: